Wage slave to financial freedom

How the right property investment strategy
helped a first-time buyer escape
from the corporate rat race

By Neil Mansell

Edited by Sarah Walker

ISBN: 978-0-9568805-0-5

This book is not intended to provide personalised legal, financial or investment advice. Readers should seek professional advice with regard to such matters as interpretation of the law, proper accounting procedures, financial planning and tax before proceeding with any property investments. The Author and the Publisher specifically disclaim any liability, loss or risk which is incurred as a consequence, directly or indirectly, of the use and application of any contents of this work.

First published in England in 2011
This edition published in England in 2014

This book is dedicated to
the people who matter most:

Sarah, Mum, Dad, Vince, Te wai nui, Violet & Temaire

Contents

Introduction

This book is the coming to fruition of an idea that was floating around for 18 months or so before I actually put finger to keyboard. Over recent years, I had the privilege of sharing the story of my property investing journey with other novice and aspiring investors, and I have usually received common feedback that people really want to know more about exactly what I've done, what I got wrong, what lessons I learned, what I would do differently, etc. While it's a pleasure to speak to people personally, there is only one of me so I figured that the best way to get those answers out there would be to become an author.

In the last couple of years I have become a regular reader myself, especially of autobiographies of business people and sportsmen and business / personal development books, such as *Rich Dad, Poor Dad, The E-Myth, The Dip* and many others. These books have taught me so much and given me so many different ideas, inspiring me to continue my journey, that the idea of writing my own book and potentially inspiring others to follow my path really excites me.

I'm not a big fan of the phrase that you hear from a lot of people that have had some success - "If I can do it, anyone can do it!" – because it's simply not true. I believe that there are many reasons why people are successful and others are not, and there are a number of core traits that are 'must haves' if you are to succeed. I'll touch on many of these factors throughout this book and hopefully give you a clear understanding of who I am, how I have developed along the way – personally and as a businessman - and enjoyed the benefits of learning from others, not making the same mistakes they did and, in some cases, improving on their results!

One of my friends and mentors, Nick Carlile, often talks about me at events and describes me by saying, "There is nothing special about Neil." What an introduction! What he means, of course, is that I wasn't born with any extraordinary talents that have given me a particular advantage over anyone else. There are many more successful people than me in the world, but what I have is a real dedication, focus and commitment to consistent action-taking that, with continual learning from others and some pure hard work, has really delivered some impressive results. That's not only in the world of property, but also in my development as a person. I don't believe you can have one without the other, as to be bigger and better in the property investment business, you need to continually develop yourself and your knowledge, so that you can effectively put new learning into practice.

This is not an autobiography, but I think it's important to talk a bit about my upbringing, education and experiences as a youngster, to help you understand how I got to the point where I wanted to get involved in property and was able to choose a new path. Who I was before I started investing went a long way to giving me the drive to be able to take some big decisions that could have gone either way... but ultimately have worked out superbly well for me.

Early days...

I was born in December 1978 in Poole General hospital in Dorset. My parents owned and ran a hotel in the small town of Swanage until I was 10 years old. Living in the back of a hotel for the first 10 years of my life was a really interesting upbringing and exposed me to the world of work from a very early age. Seeing the time, hard work, commitment and dedication to customer service that my parents put into practice every day really shaped my thinking in these areas and certainly rubbed off on me. I even started helping out in the hotel with very basic jobs - delivering newspapers to the hotel guests, watering the plants and washing up - and this probably gave me the ethic for hard work, plus I had the benefit of seeing a hotel business from behind the scenes.

I got on reasonably well at school, was always in or near the top groups for most subjects and I actually liked it. I continued my education through GCSEs, to A-Levels, to eventually qualifying from Anglia Ruskin University in Chelmsford, Essex, with a 2:1 Business Studies Degree.

Throughout this time, from as early as I can remember, I was kicking a football around. Football was my main sport and my real passion, and still is. I regularly played for the school and for my local team in Swanage at all youth levels, up to the men's first team. I think I played in every position on the football pitch and often captained the team I was playing for. I wasn't a particularly vocal captain, but was always one of the better players and preferred to lead by example.

Successfully playing a team sport gives you many attributes that can become core strengths, such as teamwork, hard work, supporting your colleagues, recognising your strengths and weaknesses and making sure your own performance is as good as it can be. The key to transferring these skills effectively into other areas of your life is recognising their value and understanding that they really do apply to virtually every other field.

It was when I started playing men's football at the age of 14 that I met someone who had a massive influence on me – and my property investment career – and who eventually made me realise I had the potential to be successful in any area I chose. I'll talk more about him in Chapter 2.

After my parents sold their hotel, my Dad got involved in property investment and development but, only being in my early teens, I didn't really take any notice of the details of how it was done. Even so, seeing the physical transformation of houses and flats from the refurbishments, conversions and new build projects that he undertook gave me a real interest in property, although my appetite for it wasn't to come to the surface for a few years yet.

Getting on the corporate ladder...

I think I always had an entrepreneurial streak within me, but I was one of those people that didn't know what they wanted to be when they grew up. Then, when I did grow up, I never really knew how to do anything about it.

So, after graduating from university in 2001, I began what I thought would be my journey to riches in the corporate world. My first proper job was actually in the public sector, working for a Local Authority in Essex in the world of Economic Development, and it was certainly an 'interesting' experience. I had been there for about 6 months when a colleague in a neighbouring department, who was at the other end of the working life spectrum to me, in his final year before retirement, asked if he could give me some advice. He told me to make sure I wasn't still in that same job or working for the local authority for more than three years, otherwise it was likely I would be there for life.

I took his advice to heart and left after two and half years to start climbing another corporate ladder within an organisation in the bright lights of London. It was a few years before I realised that my ladder was leaning up against the wrong wall and I had to jump off.

I remember having an earnings target in my head, which was to make sure that my salary was always more than my age - at 24 I wanted to be earning more than £24,000 a year and then, when I got to 50, to make sure I was earning more than £50,000. It seems crazy to me now that I had those sorts of targets and I have since set much bigger, much more challenging targets for myself. But when you're in that corporate world of employment, running hard just to try not to stand still, it's easy for your priority to become simply to survive and to have as easy a life as possible.

Unfortunately, the common trap that it's all too easy for people in this kind of position to fall into, is earning more money only to spend more money. Overall, they end up taking on more debt or spending as much as they earn, and even though it may feel like they are making progress, because they have longer or more expensive holidays or update their car more often, they never really make any progress in terms of their net worth. Their lifestyle continuing in that way is dependent on going to work every day, and many are living month-to-month. Something made me realise that being on this treadmill was never going to make me truly rich.

Fortunately, that entrepreneurial/business streak in me was always at the back of my head. I kept looking around for ideas or ways to do something different but just couldn't find *the* idea, the thing that would inspire me to make a change. Like most people, I thought that winning the lottery would be the easiest and quickest way out, even though I forgot to buy a ticket most weeks!!

Looking back, all the signs pointing towards my future were there. During my student days I had lived in Halls of Residence and shared houses with many of my friends, and I always enjoyed watching TV programmes about business people and property, like *Property Ladder* and *Location, Location, Location,* yet it never occurred to me that it would or could be the business for me. Despite my Dad's previous experiences that had given me an interest in the world of property, the different houses that I had lived in and rented and the explosion of property development and investment programmes, books and articles, I just didn't know that it was possible for me to get involved and make a success of it.

...and getting ready to jump off that ladder!

The continual cycle of getting up early, driving to the office, spending time with colleagues and bosses that I didn't really like or get along with, and then driving home again for an evening in front of the TV was starting to get me down. I was fed up of being told what to do and where to be, at what time, by people that I had little respect for and who, in my opinion, were overpaid for the role that they performed. I didn't seem to be making any progress in the organisation and the route for advancement was not particularly clear. That becomes a bit depressing after a while.

Most people usually decide to make a change, or do something different, when they experience more 'pain' than they can handle - the desire to get away from their current situation is so strong that they are almost forced to make the change. There was a lot of frustration building up for me, but I was beginning to see how things could be different if I made some changes to my life.

In my day job, I was working with local business owners, and their enthusiasm for their businesses was definitely an inspiration to me. I knew that I had always ultimately wanted to replicate what I had seen when I was growing up - my parents making a success of the business they had – and I was now spurred on by seeing successful people on the TV, reading about successful people and working with successful business owners.

Even though I had moved away to go to University, I stayed in touch with a couple of friends from back home and it was one of these friends – who I'd first met playing football over ten years earlier, and who had since become very successful in business and property - that finally helped me understand how I could get involved in property and make a success of it, just as he had. He was the catalyst for changing my initial desire to be a business owner into action - actually becoming one in practice – and finally making that big leap from the perceived safety net of employment to the more risky, but potentially infinitely more rewarding world of property.

I had a plan: my friend was going to help me replicate his success, teaching me all he had learned about property and business, and I finally felt able and confident to make the changes I needed to. And this was the start of a huge period of life-changing learning, beginning with the realisation that rather than 'more money' being my main driver - which is what I thought I was aiming for - money is simply a by-product of success. The two things all this is really about are Freedom and Choice.

PART ONE:

WAGE SLAVE TO FINANCIAL FREEDOM

Chapter 1

The Fear

Fear is something that affects everyone. One of the best descriptions I have heard is: **F**alse **E**vidence **A**ppearing **R**eal. When you think about it, most of the things we fear are not actually that bad once we experience them; it's the *thought* of them that scares the life out of us! There are loads of different things that people are scared of - driving, spiders, the dark, speaking in public, meeting new people, etc. - but usually when you speak to those that have overcome their fears, they say, "it wasn't as bad as I expected", or, "I don't know what I was really worried about".

It's said we're only born with two fears (or nervous reflexes) - loud noises and the sensation of falling – everything else we fear has been learned at some stage in our lives, and therefore we can un-learn it. Easier said than done, I know, but the point is, it *can* be done.

I have no worries about holding up my hands and telling people that, even though I had made a decision and commitment to start my property investment journey, I was scared of actually doing it. The fear that came with the thought of me doing something different and stepping out of my comfort zone was a very difficult challenge to overcome, despite the fact that it was something that I was already determined I wanted to do. Even with my previous experiences in and around the world of property, it was still a big mental obstacle right from the start to believe I could actually do it myself.

I'll talk more in Chapter 8 about my self-development, but one of the tools and techniques I learnt, which enabled me to overcome my core fear, was to set goals and commit to paper some of the things that I wanted to achieve. Goal setting is something that very successful people do on a regular basis and, over the last 4 or 5 years, it has been a key contributor to my success and become a fundamental part of my life. At that starting point, it gave me something to focus on and was a constant, visual reminder of why I wanted to get involved in property investing and what the potential rewards could be.

When I actually started investing in property at the end of 2005, that was after an eight-month journey of research. I went on courses and watched, listened to and read everything about property I could lay my hands on and, at that time, everything screamed about what a great market it was to invest in. To coin the very corny phrase that was being used at the time: "You couldn't go wrong with property". But that was one of my problems - it just seemed too good to be true. I thought it couldn't possibly be *that* easy (which it isn't!) and was worried that if I bought a house, I would buy the wrong one and make a mess of it, so I found it very hard to get started.

Keeping it to myself

I made the decision not to tell many of my friends and family what I was going to be doing, because of the fears that I had, and that's something I'd recommend to anyone about to take a similar plunge. As much as we all love our friends and family, at times they can stop us from doing the things that we really want to do. It's usually with our best interests at heart, because they don't want to see us get hurt or make any huge mistakes, but that means they'll focus on all the risks and potential downfalls. And while you should be doing enough due diligence on your new project that you find these out for yourself, you can be 100% sure they will highlight all of them for you – and probably include some myths you hadn't heard, getting themselves (and you) wound up about problems that don't really exist!

But remember that while your friends and family are giving you their opinion on what you're about to do, most of the time they won't have actually done the things that you might want to achieve. They're usually commenting and offering advice on something they have little or no experience of themselves. And sometimes the people that think they have the best advice and shout the loudest are the ones who have never achieved the scale of things in their life that you want to. Many people just don't want to see people doing things differently to them and potentially succeeding, because they've never had the confidence to step out of their own comfort zone.

The better option is to only tell people who you know will be supportive and help you overcome your fears, and to stay away from the ones who will emphasise them, because those negative people can quickly put a dampener on the flames of excitement that you'll start to experience as you get closer and closer to the point of becoming a property investor. While I was doing my research, I came across some great people – people who were successfully investing themselves, and who were taking the time to help other new investors, like me – and those were the ones I shared my goals and desires with.

Narrowing down the options

If you walk into a sweet shop and there are 100 different types of sweets to choose from, it can confuse you, especially if there are sweets you've never tried before and you don't really know which you are going to like best! Once you really look into the world of property investment and begin to understand some of the different strategies, you realise that there are a lot to choose from and it does make the decision-making process more complex. Buy to let is the most common option people think of, or 'buy, refurbish and sell', but there are many, many more, and finding out which strategy best suits your circumstances, financial plans and goals takes time. What I learned – and what I'll talk more about in the next chapter – is that the best way to decide where to start is to get advice from someone that has been there and done it before, who has no vested interest in your choices and who can advise you about all the pros and cons.

The array of options – most of which have sub-strategies – include:

- Conventional Buy to Let (BTL)
- Houses in Multiple Occupation (HMOs)
- Buying off plan
- Development / New build
- Refurbishment projects
- Commercial investments (e.g. shops, offices, warehouses, etc.)
- International investments
- Buying land
- Converting the use of properties through planning applications

Within those strategies are questions like:

- Do I buy flats or houses?
- Where do I buy them? In the town where I live or further afield?
- Which areas in those towns are in demand from tenants and where are the property prices still affordable for me?
- Do I stick to the UK or can I invest internationally & what are the pros and cons?
- Will I manage the property myself or is it better to employ the services of a letting agent?
- What type of tenants should I target? Students, professionals, families or people on Local Housing Allowance (LHA)

- Where/how do I find the best opportunities?
- Is residential or commercial investing (or both) best for me?
- Do I find the deals myself or work with another company or person to source them for me?
- Where can I find reliable contractors to do the building/refurbishment work for me?
- What finance do I need to use?
- How do I find the right specialist solicitors for my strategy/ies?
- What insurance policies do I need to take out?
- What are my exit routes if something doesn't go according to plan?

...and there are numerous others.

You can begin to see that there are many, many things to consider, but if you think about all the different options for too long you can fall into the same trap that many others have, where you get so caught up in trying to make sure you analyse the options properly, your research and due diligence starts to mushroom and you can end up never actually taking the plunge. There are people I met three or four years ago, when they were first starting to think about investing in property...and today they tell me they're still "checking out the options". This is commonly known as "Analysis Paralysis".

I wholeheartedly agree that you should do research and investigate the different strategies and opportunities, but you also have to acknowledge that you simply cannot know everything in advance. At some point you have to make that leap of faith and just get started.

In my case, I started attending a number of property investment education courses to gather information and understanding about what my options were and, I have to say, they were great for delivering that. But what they didn't do was actually help me to take that first step and I still had the fear and nagging thought in the back of my head of, "What will I do if it all goes wrong?"

Risk v Reward

When you're starting out, the fear of it all going wrong is bound to be one of your major concerns. Ultimately, everyone will have a different starting point in terms of experience, finances, etc. and so the downside for everyone will be different. My main thought process involved looking at the worst that could happen to me. Would I die? No! Would I still have a job and be earning money? Yes. Would I be a bit embarrassed that I had tried something and it didn't work out? Yes, but I would get over it. Would I lose some money? Probably, but at least I would still have a job. If no one wanted to rent the property from me, could I live there? Yes. Could I sell it, even for a loss? Yes.

But although you have to consider the worst-case scenarios, it's really important you focus on the positives and think about the difference taking this step could make to your life. I looked at the benefits and opportunities getting started in the property business would give me. Would I earn more money if I bought and rented out the right property? Yes. Would I learn a lot along the way that I could use for further property investments? Yes. Would my confidence grow as a result of making a success of my first investment? Definitely. Would it give me the taste for more? Probably.

The measurement used in most cases is the risk versus the reward ratio. We all have different risk profiles and usually those with a higher propensity to take risks don't worry about their fears. They have an attitude of simply getting on with things and seeing what happens. Sometimes it works and sometimes it doesn't! If you take a lot of risk you usually want to know in advance that the rewards are going to be worth it, however this is not always possible.

I'm sure you have friends and family members that have properties they bought 20 or 30 years ago, and now the capital values of those properties are many times higher than when they originally bought them. If they knew at the time of buying what would subsequently happen to the property market, then they would probably have bought as many as they could physically get their hands on. The rewards would have been so great that the perceived risk of buying at that time would have been negligible...but unfortunately things just don't work like that!

You can, however, minimise your risks and maximise your rewards in property by looking at what the most successful investors have done in the past and what they continue to do now. There is a great saying - 'success leaves clues' - and following a tried and tested system is one of the best ways to overcome your fears and increase your chances of success.

Sidestepping 'analysis paralysis'

Fear usually comes about because of a lack of knowledge or understanding. Something that you think *could* happen to you stops you from moving forwards and, until that fear is overcome, progress is either very slow or simply doesn't happen at all. In terms of property investing, the phrase that I like to use about myself when I was starting out is, I was 'waiting for that perfect day to come', and there are so many other people doing the same. They're waiting for the property prices to drop a little bit further before they buy...or they're waiting for a better rate on mortgages to be available or a higher loan to value product so they have to put less of their own money into the deal...or they're hanging on until they can find a seller who'll take a lower offer... *Something* is always not quite right, and until everything falls into place they just won't make that commitment to take action.

You – as I did - have to face reality and recognise that the 'perfect day' will *never* come but, nevertheless, experienced, sophisticated investors can make money in any market - you just need to be aware of the market conditions at that time and take the right action. There are so many things that are out of your control, which you have no influence over at all, so don't worry about them. Just get on with it and focus on the things that *are* within your control.

I mentioned earlier about comfort zones and really want to emphasise the importance of getting out of yours and doing new things. Every time you step out of your current comfort zone and try something that you either don't think you can do, or that scares you a little, it makes your comfort zone bigger. Those fears that you had will have been overcome and they then become an everyday part of who you are and what you do. In property investment, a great example of this is dealing with estate agents.

If you have never dealt with an estate agent before, or only had a couple of dealings on properties for you to live in yourself, when you move on to talking about pure investments they can come across in a way that makes you feel uncomfortable. Often that's because of a perceived difference in knowledge between you and the agent, and that relationship can take a while to develop. I remember my first experiences with estate agents - to be honest, I had no idea what they were talking about some of the time. Some of the words and phrases that I had never heard of really took me outside of my comfort zone, however, by simply asking questions and doing some further research I became familiar with those terms. Relatively quickly, I found I could easily engage in a conversation on the same level as them and then, after a while, even above their level!

Doing things that are unfamiliar is always a challenge, but every time you take on something new and look to push into higher levels or different areas of business or your personal life, you need to leave your comfort zone behind and get stuck into your new environment. Just remember that although there will be a period of discomfort whilst you get used to your new surroundings, you are growing your comfort zone to include that new activity or skill, until it just blends in with everything else that you are happy doing.

The fear of failure and of the unknown was such a big challenge for me to overcome initially and yet, looking back now, I don't know what I was worried about! Once you have conquered your fear of getting started, there will always be many more challenges along the way and different fears to overcome but I can honestly tell you that it gets easier the more you do it. Having gone through that initial process of getting used to stepping outside my comfort zone, I began to find that I was more confident in many different areas of my life and would take on challenges that previously I would have avoided at all costs. Over the past few years, I've run a marathon, done a skydive, learned to ski, taken on bigger and bigger refurbishment projects and accumulated multi-million pounds worth of mortgage debt. I am constantly pushing my personal fear boundaries and now look forward to conquering new challenges because of the knock-on rewards I know each one will bring me.

A great book that I highly recommend you read is *Feel the fear and do it anyway*, by Susan Jeffers. The title really does describe her take on fear and how to overcome it, and the lessons and techniques in the book can be applied to many different areas of life. Whenever you know that you are going to do something that you are scared of or fearful about, just say the words, "feel the fear and do it anyway", and you will have more confidence to take on those challenges.

While I now had a little bit of knowledge and the fear 'under control', I knew that I was also going to need a helping hand to get started. It was time to find the right guidance to help me put my plans into action.

Chapter 2

Finding the right helping hand

With my initial fears about doing something different and stepping out of my comfort zone overcome, the next step was to understand exactly what I was going to do and, most importantly, how I was going to achieve it.

The friend who ultimately got me taking the right action recommended that I went on a variety of courses to begin to learn more about what the options were, how they worked and, ultimately, to see which ones would be suitable for my situation. As a first time buyer with little property experience and only a small amount of capital to get started, it was vital that I picked a strategy that suited me and would best help me to achieve my goals.

I started out by attending free seminars and workshops on all sorts of different aspects of property investing, thinking that would be an easy and pain free way of getting going. Free events - particularly in the property investing world - tend to be taster sessions or stepping stones to more education, which then comes at a cost. The general perception of free events is that they don't have much real value, but you can actually take away some great hints and tips and make useful contacts, so I'd definitely recommend you look them out, in and around your local area. The issue for me, in my situation, was that hints and tips weren't going to help me take action in a thought out and structured way. Those free events were great for me to learn a little, but not enough for me to actually do anything about the information I was learning.

I've heard lots of stories about people that go on these free courses or events, think they have learnt all there is to know, and then go out and make a complete mess of it. They buy the wrong property in the wrong location and top it off by paying the wrong price as well! In the world of property investing, a little bit of information can be very dangerous and it's a fairly unforgiving business to be in when you get things wrong. In one way, though, I actually take my hat off to those people because they were clearly able to set any fears aside and put what they had learned straight into practice. They took a 'Ready-Fire-Aim' approach, jumped in and then sorted out their problems afterwards, rather than the 'Ready-Aim-Fire' approach that I had to take, as I simply couldn't afford to get it wrong on my first property.

Realising free events weren't going to get me to where I needed to be, I decided that events or courses that actually cost some money would probably be a better way to go. Over a 6 month period I paid several thousand pounds to attend a variety of one day and weekend courses, which was a big investment for me. Looking back now, I feel like I was taking the easy option because there would always be this 'get out clause' of being able to blame the people that ran the course if something went wrong or if they didn't teach me everything I needed to know! In reality, I was still making progress and was certainly learning lots about property investing, but although the knowledge I was getting was great, I still just wasn't brave enough to put it into action.

We've all heard the phrase, 'Knowledge is Power', but that's not quite accurate. It's the *application* of knowledge that is the most powerful thing. I had lots of knowledge, but wasn't able to apply it, and what's the point in learning what to do or learning what other successful people have done if you don't then take action and follow in their footsteps? A person having knowledge and not applying it is much worse than someone not doing anything simply because they don't know any different...and I was in danger of becoming that person!

Something like 95% of people that attend paid-for events or intensive courses walk away from them really psyched up and ready to go, but as soon as they leave that environment and get back into the real world, they get absorbed in their daily lives and usual distractions and any momentum that has been built up is soon lost. It really can be a case of two steps forward and then two steps back.

One reason for this is that many of these events and training courses are regularly attended by anything up to 150 people. With that number of aspiring investors in one room, all with different financial situations, abilities, knowledge and goals, it's virtually impossible to get the specific help or answers that you need and advice that's applicable to your personal, individual situation. The training also tends to be delivered in such a way that there is just enough information to enable you to get started, but not enough time to go into all the detail that is really needed. As a result, while you may feel able to buy a property and make that start, you can be pretty certain that you'll get stuck at some point and then you may not be sure where to go for help.

You also need to beware of the sales element – I certainly found the actual 'sales process' involved in some of the courses I went on quite scary. Usually part of each day was focused specifically on getting you to upgrade to the next workshop or event they were organising or, in some cases, even encouraging you to buy property from them there and then. Sometimes the money required to go on the next course was even more than I had put aside to actually put towards a property and yet there was no apparent interest in me, personally, or my individual situation. I was just a number or a face in the room that they wanted to sell to – whether or not it was the right thing for me was irrelevant. A number of the companies that employed the worst of these 'sales tactics' no longer exist, but I'm sure if you're into property investing you will probably have been on similar courses or attended the same sort of events. That business model is one of quantity versus quality and as long as you could afford it (and even if you couldn't, you were encouraged to pay for it on a credit card!) then they would take your money and promise to do great things with it. Fortunately, I knew enough to realise that approach was not for me and I walked away.

Whether property education costs money or not, the real measure you should use is the value that you get from it. Courses and seminars on their own very rarely deliver the results that people need, but they are great ways to learn. Actually putting the information into practice on your own is the difficult part. I still attend a number of courses and events every year to learn from other people, fully aware of their limitations in terms of what they can and can't do for me. *Please* make sure that you go to any seminars, courses, etc. with your eyes wide open; take the learning from them but also understand where that one type of learning sits in the wider spectrum of help and support that you can get.

A very helpful piece of advice...

My friend, Steve Bolton, was in the very early stages of setting up his own property investor mentoring business when I was trying to get started, and I regularly spoke to him about what I was learning on the courses. He'd attended some of the same courses himself and I was very keen to learn from him because he was actually putting what he had learned into practice and was building up a portfolio of properties in his home town of Bournemouth, down on the south coast. He was making some mistakes along the way but, overall, making a great success of it. We spoke about my own situation in more detail and he gave me probably the single best piece of advice I could have had at that time to help me make a decision about which way to go. He told me I had to work out what I wanted to do in life and then see which property strategy I should implement to help me get there, rather than deciding what seemed to be the best thing to do in property and then seeing whether it fitted in with my life.

For me (as I think it would be for most people) that was a very interesting and different way of looking at property investment. So many investors focus on what will give them the biggest 'profit' (usually a promise of X% equity growth) but that may involve things like investing overseas or getting into property development, and for some people that turns out not to suit their situation and they end up with a hobby of buying properties that give them more problems than they ever really wanted. Chasing the best deals around the country or around the world is completely the wrong foundation on which to build a successful and sustainable property business and can have a massive negative impact on people - personally, financially and in terms of family life.

So I spent some time really thinking about what I wanted to do in the next 2-3 years. It was a really great exercise, as I'd never thought seriously about that sort of thing – I just assumed time would gradually carry me up the corporate ladder - and it helped me to prioritise different things. I came to the conclusion that I wanted to either run my own business or be self-employed. The main issue was that I couldn't afford to give up my 9-5 job, so I decided I would focus on building up my income stream from property part-time, whilst holding down the day-job until I could afford to quit and focus on property full-time.

I enjoyed parts of my job, which was essentially working with businesses based in East London and helping them access grants and business support, but I would often get frustrated at the culture in the company and what I saw as a lack of quality in the Management. With no clear path for changing that or getting promotion, it soon became clear that my desire to leave was greater than any desire to progress with the company, but I recognised that I would just have to sit tight for a while until I could afford to go it alone.

A major turning point for me was an annual review with my boss, where I clearly remember him saying, "Neil, you have no future working at this organisation, so if you want to make any progress or get promotion, you will have to leave". Not quite what I was expecting - I was hoping for some positive comments! - but whilst his words initially came as a bit of a shock to me, they gave me that determination, focus and commitment to actually go out there, take control of my own destiny and not allow other people to have an influence on my future. Sometimes the truth hurts, but I'm actually really glad that he pointed out that I was going nowhere with my existing career, because he did me a huge favour.

By this time I had already been on a couple of courses, and with that spark of change burning within me I was now ready to take action and begin my property investing journey.

On some of the courses I had attended I had begun to learn about an investment strategy called HMOs (Houses in Multiple Occupation). These are properties that have multiple tenants living in them, whether that be a block of flats, hotel or an individual house. As a youngster I had grown up living in the back of a hotel and as a student I had lived in halls of residence, as well as renting a room in a house and sharing houses with my friends. I had been the end user of an HMO but never, ever thought about it as an investment opportunity or considered that I might eventually be a provider of that kind of accommodation. It was, however, the most suitable strategy for me to begin with, as the main reason for buying these sorts of properties is to generate monthly cash flow. I needed to replace my employed salary as soon as possible and, in the majority of cases, the traditional buy to let model just doesn't offer that. My basic plan was to focus on investing in property whenever I wasn't at work, until the surplus income from those properties replaced my salary and I could quit my job. Now that was a great driving force and goal to have, considering the statement my boss had made at my last annual review, but I would have to hold back on writing the resignation letter for the moment.

I continued to read books about property investing and learn about other people who had been successful, and when I next spoke to Steve, I told him about what my boss had said to me and how that made me feel. I think it was at that point we both knew the time had come for me to go out and become a property investor!

Mentoring

Steve told me more about the mentoring company he'd developed in order to be able to effectively help people put into practice what they had learned and provide some longer term support, or to learn a different way of investing if they were already property investors. Mentoring in the world of property investing was a relatively new concept at that time and any sort of mentoring was completely new to me.

The basic principle is that you have someone who has been there and done it before, teaching you their methods on a one to one basis and helping you to put into practice what they have done themselves, effectively replicating their success. The one to one element enables you to go at the right speed for you, in an environment where you feel comfortable asking questions and learning something new. It's also vital that you like and trust your mentor, as you're going to be spending a lot of time together and following their lead in situations that may be initially foreign and uncomfortable for you. With a number of years of friendship behind us and having seen the success Steve had made of his property business, which had HMOs at its core, I knew I would be in safe hands with him as my mentor.

There were two main reasons I thought that mentoring would work well for me. Firstly, I was going to be taking on a lot of new information and would be well outside my comfort zone, so having someone there who could 'hand hold' me when I needed it gave me a much-needed confidence boost. And secondly, I knew I would benefit hugely from having someone that would also make me accountable to them (i.e. I'd actually have to get things done!) and be able to give me a kick of encouragement now and again when things were not going to plan. I was not a leader or someone that easily came up with a business idea, but if I was given a system to follow or a framework in which to operate I felt I certainly had the potential to be a success. With a mentor, I could learn directly from someone who was successful at the strategy they were teaching and leverage their credibility with local professional advisors. Back then, the thought of approaching estate agents on my own, as a first time buyer with no experience of investing (apart from going on a few courses), was pretty scary.

The agents would have eaten me alive!

One to one mentoring usually costs a lot more than going on a course with 100 other people, so the investment I was making in myself had to work this time. I knew I absolutely had to take action and make that initial investment look small compared to the results I would get from putting the information and learning into practice. The cost was relatively high but the value I would get if I followed the system would far outweigh that. Suddenly the prize of winning was greater than the fear of losing.

I was ready to become a HMO property investor in my hometown of Chelmsford, Essex. My mentoring dates were booked in for 11th & 12th September 2005 and I had plenty of research to do before then. I had written down some basic goals, identified the right investment strategy, found someone to help and support me and I was mentally ready to take on a new challenge. It was finally all becoming a reality.

Chapter 3

Getting up the first few rungs of the ladder

With fairly limited knowledge but a burning desire to get started, under Steve's guidance I began properly researching my local town of Chelmsford. Although I had lived there for a number of years and knew about the town in general, I had no real knowledge of the property market and the drivers and influences behind it. I began to look into things like local employment opportunities and who the major employers were; how many commuters were travelling into London each day; if there were any major regeneration projects planned; how many people were employed in the public sector (schools, hospitals, etc.); historical statistics of how the property market had performed; where any new housing developments were happening, and so on. This then fed into looking online at actual properties and getting an understanding of local prices and typically how much different types of properties cost, what they would rent for, which areas were in high demand from tenants and where to avoid (i.e. which areas had the best and worst reputations!). These days, there is so much information online regarding area statistics that you can get swamped in all the numbers, however it is very important to gain a general understanding if you're serious about becoming a professional investor. The key is to make sure you're aware of the numbers and issues relevant to your strategy, but not get stuck in the trap of over-analysing the information.

I wasn't an expert overnight but I soon found myself becoming familiar with the area and had a basic understanding of how the local market worked. Over time, I would become an expert and – even down to street level – be able to tell you where to invest and where to avoid and confidently assess the value of different properties in different areas. I used to buy the local newspaper every week, take out the property supplement, cover up the prices of the properties that were advertised for sale and, just from the basic details you get on each listing, try to guess how much they were being marketed at. It might not sound like an exciting game but it soon helped me become incredibly knowledgeable about prices in Chelmsford.

I was doing this research in the evenings and at weekends, around my full time job, and this was to become a familiar pattern for the early days of my investing journey. I can't emphasise enough the importance of dedicating time to doing this kind of research. If you're seriously committed to making things work, you need to allocate enough time to give you the best chance of success. And when you really look at your life, you'll probably be amazed at how much time you spend in an ordinary week doing things of very little consequence. I became more disciplined with my time, made lists of what I had to achieve every day and I stopped watching television in the evenings. In short, I began to use my time more effectively and productively, and I'll talk more about how you can do this yourself in the next chapter.

The Money

In preparation for my two one-to-one mentoring days with Steve I researched and collected my credit rating report, spoke to a mortgage broker about my ability to access mortgages and made sure that I had my money in an accessible place, ready for when we found my first property. My initial pot of funds to buy property was very limited. I wasn't earning a huge salary but my living costs were fairly low and over the previous few years I had put aside some money 'for a rainy day' - and now the day had come to put it to good use.

At the end of 2005, when I began investing in property, mortgages were fairly easy to access. When property prices are rising, the lenders see little risk in handing out high loan to value (LTV) mortgages because almost as soon as they have lent money against property it has gone up in value. That means if they ever need to repossess the property, they can be confident it will have enough equity to allow them to easily reclaim the money they have lent. I was fortunate to begin investing at this time, when the levels of deposit required were minimal or, in some cases, none.

It was very common to be able to get a 95% mortgage, and do you remember the '125% LTV mortgages' being offered by some banks? Those were, essentially, two-part financing, made up of a mortgage for 90% or 95% of the property's value plus an unsecured loan for the balance. (The loan part did not fall under FSA regulation). They were most often given to people who planned to make significant improvements to a property, but were also given to some people who were in a negative equity situation with their current property and needed to move up the ladder but couldn't quite stretch. That kind of lending has been widely criticised as irresponsible but, for investors who knew what they were doing and had solid revenue-generating buy to let systems in place, the ready availability of financing was a real bonus.

In those days, I didn't really know how mortgages and finance worked, and this was just one area in my investment journey that was a steep learning curve for me. Fortunately, one of the benefits of working with someone who has been there and done it before is that they will have some good contacts you should be able to use and, in property investing, having a good mortgage broker as part of your team is vital. They can make a huge difference between helping you access funds for certain deals that will make you lots of money and missing out on deals because you can't get the right finance in the right timeframe.

As a student going through university, I had used a credit card or two to support my living expenses but I was not reckless, always made at least the minimum repayments and tried to clear off the balance in full whenever possible. Little was I aware that this track record of borrowing and repaying money would help me access finance in the future. Borrowing money is seen by many people to be a bad thing but, in terms of your credit rating, having a proven history of borrowing and paying back the money is what will give banks and other lending institutions the confidence to lend when you really need it – like getting a mortgage. It was news to me to learn that people that have a lot of debt but make regular repayments will have a better credit rating than those that don't use things like credit cards.

Please understand that I am not advocating you go out and spend wildly on a credit card just to boost your credit rating, but showing evidence that you can borrow money and repay it will stand you in good stead. Basic living expenses, like your weekly food shop or filling up the car, can be put on a credit card and then paid off in full at the end of the month. Credit cards are an expensive form of debt if you allow balances to grow but, used sensibly, they will enhance your credit rating and do come in useful at times. More on this later in the chapter.

I mentioned that my general living costs were low. At the time, I was living with two of my friends, renting a property that was going to be demolished, as it was next to a major redevelopment site. As such, the owners had not spent a lot of money on it in recent years, so we were getting a very cheap rent. I was, however, soon to move in with my girlfriend for the first time, so I expected my living expenses to rise shortly after that! Analysing my own expenditure was an interesting exercise and something that, if you haven't done it before, I would highly recommend you do right away. It's amazing how much money we waste each month and actually analysing this and putting it into a spreadsheet really emphasised to me how I could save a bit more and then put those savings towards my property investments.

Getting down to it

It was September 2005 when my friend Steve came to spend two days with me in Chelmsford, to help me put into practice all the research I'd been doing. This was the next stage of investment of my time and money: I took time off work and, even though he was a friend, Steve charged me for his time. Now, you might initially think this was a bit unfair of him, but it would have been unfair for me to expect him to spend his valuable time with me for nothing. Actually paying for the mentoring made me realise the value it had and the value of Steve's time, and made me recognise that to get a return on that investment I would need to go out and put into practice what I was being taught. If it had been free, then I wouldn't have had anything to lose if I hadn't taken action afterwards; I wouldn't have really felt accountable to myself or Steve. Paying for knowledge and support was actually the very best thing I could have done.

I've already talked about the fear I had at the start, but beginning the mentoring process was actually very exciting. It was suddenly so real - I was finally going to start doing what I had wanted to do now for many months. The one thing that did frighten me again was when Steve asked if I would be comfortable with multi-millions of pounds of mortgage debt! I had never owed anyone more than a few hundred pounds, so the thought of millions of pounds of debt was pretty scary. However, I knew I would have to accept it if I was going to be successful in the world of property investing and soon understood that as long as the value of the assets was greater than the value of the debt and the income from the assets outweighed the repayments of the debt, then I would be in a positive position. It really was like a game of monopoly but in real life!

We began to implement the same system that Steve was using to source and buy his properties down on the South

Coast. I had never spoken to an estate agent before, viewed any properties (other than online) or knew what to ask or look for in a property, so Steve led the way on most of it. I listened and learned and then tried to do what he was doing. It really is the best way to learn, with the benefit that you're getting results at the same time. Understanding the theory of how to do things is great, but we remember most of what we learn by actually doing it and putting the theory into practice. I made some mistakes in what I said to agents, and what I did and didn't ask, but I then got immediate feedback from Steve so I had a better idea of what to do next time. And as we were packing a lot into the two days, I had plenty of chances to practice and refine my patter! As I made progress, Steve would take me through the next steps, and so on.

Over the two days we viewed about 10 properties that, on paper, looked like they might fit my criteria. As I had hardly any property experience, one of things I wanted to find was a property that worked in terms of the numbers, but that also was going to be relatively small and easy for me to learn on. One of the properties was a ground floor maisonette in a road that I used to live in, that would give me four lettable rooms. Remember, my strategy was to buy properties that could be HMOs (Houses in Multiple Occupation) and, in the model we were using, 4 lettable rooms was really the least that you would need to make a big enough difference in the income levels compared to a normal single occupancy tenanted property.

The maisonette was owned by a landlord already who had rented it out previously. It was a little dated and what you might call a 'typical' tenanted property, however the layout and structure were ideal for me. The landlord's family had already emigrated to Australia and he couldn't join them until he had the money from the sale of this property. We identified that there may be an opportunity for 'a deal' due to the time pressure being greater than the money pressure. After about a week of negotiating, we agreed a sale price and also agreed a deal which involved a 'gifted deposit'. Up until around 2007, creative financing techniques were relatively easy to use in the property investing world. The Financial Services Authority said that the maximum allowance, or incentive, that you could build into a deal was 5% of the value of the property. You could tailor a deal so that the 5% was used in such a way that it reduced the amount of capital you were required to put into a deal yourself, effectively increasing the amount of borrowing on a property.

I would need a whole chapter to explain this in more detail, but it was a way that I could make my pot of investment funds go further. In my circumstances, this creative financing technique was vital to the deal. Again, with Steve's help, the deal was put together and so I learnt an advanced way of investing in property in a safe but real environment. Mentoring had accelerated my learning, which in turn saved me a whole lot of money on deposit funds, and I had the peace of mind of knowing that I was working alongside an expert who wouldn't let me make any significant mistakes.

Towards the end of the second day of mentoring it suddenly dawned on me that Steve was going to go back home and I would be here on my own trying to continue what we had started. I had taken in a massive amount of information in a very short period of time and felt so far out of my comfort zone that part of me wanted to go back to how it was previously, before I set the wheels in motion on the biggest single purchase of my life, which would land me with the most debt I'd ever had in my life! I've since found this is a common response to any situation where you do something completely new and it's often referred to as 'the dip'.

Any learning curve is exactly what is says: a curve, not just a straight line upwards. There is a great book I would recommend you read, actually called *The Dip*, written by Seth Godin, and it explains this situation very clearly. The downwards part of the curve was exactly where I felt I was and, despite making great leaps forward, I actually felt uncomfortable in my new environment. But when you understand how 'the dip' works, you begin to recognise the stages you go through when you do something new and different from before, and learn to react accordingly. Now when I do new things that are slightly uncomfortable for me at first, I understand the process going on in my head and can rationalise any fears before they take hold. Really, read that book – it makes a lot of sense.

From 'sale agreed' to 'up and running'!

In terms of the property, I was now sale agreed and had to instruct the solicitors and mortgage brokers to do their part of the transaction. Again, having tried and tested people I could call on to explain the process so I understood what was happening, as well as them just getting on with it, was of great help to me. Looking back, I cringe at some of the really stupid questions I asked them, but they weren't stupid to me at the time. While I didn't really understand a lot of what was happening, I do credit myself with being a quick learner. I only need to ask or be told something once before it sticks with me, so at least I didn't ask those stupid questions over and over again!

I also spent some time with Steve putting together an action plan of things for me to do over the coming weeks and months that would help me achieve my goals of becoming a successful investor and starting to build up an income stream from property. I agreed to send him a progress report at the end of each week detailing what I had been up to, and being accountable to someone really helped me stay focused. I don't know if he read them or not, but that process of recording my activity was a great stick to beat myself with – there was no point in sending Steve a progress report with nothing on it! Completing the actions and activities detailed in my progress report was only possible through dedicating time to it during evenings and weekends, around my day job. I started watching TV less, especially the soap operas, and instead spent time on the internet doing more research, contacting people and generally keeping up the momentum. When I finally became the proud owner of my first property, in December 2005, I also then sacrificed much of the time I spent on one of my real passions, football. I had played for years and had joined a team locally but, when I had property work to do, football then came second. Up until that point I would have not put football behind anything, but I knew I wouldn't be giving it up forever, only for a short period of time, while I got my first property up to scratch and ready to be rented out.

Once I had taken ownership of the property, the next challenge I had was to find local tradesmen that could do the refurbishment work for me. I decided the best way was to try and get recommendations or referrals, so I simply started asking friends if they knew of anyone. I soon began to build up some contacts – plumbers, electricians, builders, etc. – and, again, I benefitted from Steve's experience in knowing what things should cost and how long they should take to do, rather than running the risk of being taken for a ride. I decided I was going to do as many of the basic labouring jobs I could, myself, and that I would also be the painter / decorator and handyman, building all the new flat pack furniture that we would get for the house. With HMO properties, tenants tend to expect them to be fully furnished, so I was going to be spending a lot of time with an Allen key! My girlfriend helped me greatly and we spent many hours painting and building the furniture together, while our friends were out drinking and socialising. I was 26 at the time, so that was hard to do, but I just kept focused on my end goal of earning enough money from property to enable me to leave my full-time job. It was sometimes hard to stay focused, but I soon found that if the end prize is big enough and you want it enough, it's not hard to do.

We actually refurbished and furnished the property within about one month and, on Steve's advice, started to look for tenants while we were still doing the work. I advertised in the local newspaper and online and was inundated with enquiries.

I did 5 viewings and filled the 4 rooms before the property was even finished. Now I was on my way up and out of the dip that I had experienced during my mentoring, as everything looked rosy and people really wanted to live in my property!

If no one had wanted to live there, I did have a back-up plan – I would have lived there myself, instead of in the flat that we rented. I had lived in that street previously and, while it wasn't my dream home, it would have been a good start. But, happily, the back-up wasn't needed. My 4 new tenants all paid me a deposit to secure their room and paid their monthly rent in advance when they moved in. All the hard work had been worthwhile and I felt like a success. Everything Steve had told me was going to happen, did, and I was now the owner of a property with tenants paying me for the privilege of living there.

My girlfriend, Sarah, and I went out to celebrate at a local restaurant. Celebrating any successes you have is important. What's the point in setting yourself goals or targets if you don't celebrate the achievement of meeting or exceeding them? It is recognition of your hard work and means you will look forward to setting your next set of goals so you can celebrate meeting those ones as well.

You may be surprised that I only told my parents what I had been up to once the property was fully tenanted and they were quite shocked to hear about what had really been going on in my life for the past few months. Although my Dad had been involved in property previously, he was not aware that professional people would want to house share and how it made sense as an investment strategy to offer that sort of accommodation - even to a seasoned property investor it was a new experience. I had told a few colleagues at work and some of my friends what I was doing, and they were generally interested in what I was up to, but I think some of them were waiting for it to all fall down around me. How wrong they would be! Over the years, a few of them have told me how they wish they'd done what I did back then but think they have missed the opportunity. My response is that there is always an opportunity to do something about it; it just depends on how committed you are.

Getting the bug

With the first house now up and running and any early teething problems sorted out, I really wanted to go out and do it again. I could see why people said that buying property can become addictive. The lure of finding the next deal and putting it together is what really drives some people, whatever sector or industry they work in, and property is no different. To me, having one property was a massive step up and I was thrilled I was finally on the property ladder, but wouldn't it sound much better if I could say I had two houses and not just one? One just didn't sound enough to be called an investor.

It was around March of 2006 that I went out on my own looking for another property, without Steve by my side this time, but fully armed with the knowledge that I had gained on my mentoring. I also knew he was only at the end of the phone if I needed advice. I had a little bit of confidence that I knew (a) what I was talking about and (b) what I was looking for.

And after just a few viewings I found what I thought would be a great HMO property, this time with 6 lettable rooms. It needed a lot more work than the first property, but by now I had some contacts that had done some of the work on that one and who I knew could help out with this property.

After some negotiation backwards and forwards, I secured my second property. It wasn't until I picked up the keys and went back to look at what I had bought that it really begun to sink in how much work was required. My role again was to be the general labourer, the painter/decorator and builder of all things that came as flat pack furniture. For a solid 7 week period this was my daily schedule: Leave for work in London at 7.15am, get back home at 6pm and then be at the property from 6.30pm – 11pm every day, Monday to Friday, spending 14-16 hours there on both Saturday and Sunday!! I had no social life, gave up playing football temporarily, didn't watch any TV, hardly saw my girlfriend (unless she came to the house to see me) and listened to the radio playing in the background more than I ever had in my life. It was not glamorous, it was very hard work and, at times, very lonely.

This wasn't what I had signed up for! The world of property investing was meant to be lucrative and you just paid other people to do the jobs that you couldn't do, surely? One of my issues was that I simply wasn't in the financial position to be able to pay lots of other people but, actually, it was a great way of understanding and learning in great detail what needed to be done to a property to make it into an HMO. I now look back on that situation and can see how it would have been easy to give up, try to cut corners and just get it over and done with, but I'm so glad I stuck at it and put in the time and effort, because I have certainly reaped the rewards. My big lesson from that experience was that there will always be times when we have to do things we don't want to do, in order to get to the places that we want to get to. Having my goals and targets set firmly in my brain kept my spirits up and I knew that the end would soon be in sight – I just had to keep going.

Pretty much as per the first property, all the rooms were let either before I had finished most of the work or very shortly after the house was officially ready. That feeling of someone giving me money as a deposit to secure the room, and then rent to live in it, was a great reward for all the hard work that I'd put in. The tenants also made some very nice comments about the house and how lovely it looked. It's amazing how something as simple as a nice comment can make the weight of those 7 weeks of hard graft almost disappear! With finances being as tight as they were, I actually paid for most of the furniture in the house on a credit card and then repaid the debt as quickly as possible from the rents I was receiving. Again, I would stress that I'm in no way advocating reckless spending on credit cards, but I am trying to emphasise how you can be creative and use alternative solutions to help you along the way. At the time there were plenty of 0% interest deals around and so it made sense to use those to finance the cost of the furniture.

Finding more money and hitting the accelerator

Now I had run out of money completely. I can't tell you how frustrated I felt, knowing I had a system and model that quite clearly worked and could see plenty of fantastic potential deals out there, but simply didn't have any money to take advantage of the situation. But Steve had always told me that if you have a really great deal, you can usually find the money from somewhere, so I kept looking, and around October 2006 I found a property that would be ideal as my next investment.

The next stage of my journey was to begin to look around for other investors that would be interested in putting up the money for a great return. I was relatively confident that I could show them how I had already spent my own money on something that worked and was operating a solid system, but now needed more capital to take it to the next level and turn it into a real business. I put together a very basic business plan outlining how much money I needed, how much profit it would generate, how I could pay the money back and what interest rate I could offer on the money.

I approached someone who I knew had funds that they put into a range of investments and who I thought would be interested in investing into property. My hunch was right - they were receptive from the start and keen to learn more about what I was proposing. With lots more discussion we reached an agreement that they would effectively fund all the capital required, get that capital back within a specified period of time and I would pay them a good rate of interest in the meantime. It was a deal that worked for both parties: a win-win. Their confidence in me came from seeing the two existing properties that I had up and running and the various spreadsheets demonstrating how they were performing. To get outside investment it's absolutely vital you run your properties as a business and not just a hobby, so it really helped that I genuinely enjoyed looking at all the numbers and keeping a close eye on how things were going.

You probably won't be surprised to hear that the 3rd house needed even more work doing to it! By now I was getting more and more confident and was happy to take on new challenges. My comfort zone had grown massively and I was always on the lookout for new opportunities and ever-more creative ways to buy properties and turn them into HMOs. The fears I had at the start had disappeared completely and I was now just looking forwards.

The refurbishment side of things got underway at property number three and I was now really struggling to balance the time I spent at work with getting all the things done I wanted to in my property business. Quite often I would duck out into meeting rooms to take calls from existing or prospective tenants, make arrangements with tradesmen and search on the internet for new suppliers or further properties. This was the stuff that I really wanted to do and my day job was getting in the way!! But I still wasn't quite at the point where I could earn enough money from the properties to live, although I knew once the third property was up and running, I would be. Although it wouldn't be quite the same income level as my day job, it was enough, so the end was in sight.

Again, I went into that period of being at the property a lot during the evenings and at weekends, but this time I had budgeted for someone to do the decorating and for someone to build the flat pack furniture. I was still doing the general running around and project managing but at least I was slightly less involved this time, which was a great relief. Yet again, after most of the work had been completed I started showing tenants around the rooms, which, again, were in high demand. Tenants seem to love things that are new - even though the house often looked like a building site, they wanted to be the first people to live there because they could see how it would look when it was finished. The 3rd house was full pretty much as soon as the tradesmen had cleared up and left.

Ideally, I would have got a 4th property up and running before I left employment, just to be sure that there was enough money coming in. With property, if you don't have tenants you don't have a source of income and I was aware that if some rooms became empty the profit levels would quickly shrink and could disappear. Although I have never had that problem, it is something you need to be aware of and budget for. I was still in regular contact with Steve and I remember having the conversation with him about my situation. Being much more decisive than me, he helped push me towards self-employment, so I ended up resigning sooner than I really expected. It's all too easy to keep plodding along, waiting for the next deal to happen, and it's often difficult to get out of that trap of hanging around in jobs, waiting for the next bonus or pay rise. More often than not, it never happens when or as we expect and we then just hold on for the following year to be better.

It wasn't so difficult for me, though, as my boss had already made it clear to me that I had no future in the company. I plucked up the courage to arrange a meeting with him to hand in my resignation, which I think came as a bit of a shock, especially when I told him what I had been up to for the past

12 months and what I was planning to do in the future. Anyway, with one month's notice, I left employment on 11th January 2007 - a date that will stick in my mind for the rest of my life. There was no looking back and I was starting the next stage of the journey in my property investing life.

Suddenly I realised I was going to be responsible for earning my own money and had given up my entitlement to annual leave, sick pay, pension plans, etc. because I had become my own boss. I can clearly remember the last few days in employment, the feeling of nervousness about whether it was the right decision and wondering how it would all work out. Then someone said to me that if it didn't work out, I could always just go and get a job with someone else. It may not have been what I actually wanted to do, but it made me realise I couldn't lose.

I was fortunate to get out of the rat race at the age of 28 and at a relatively low salary level. I had spent a long time looking at what my general income and outgoings were and at what I actually *needed* to earn to live. What I needed to earn and what I actually earned were two different numbers. We become accustomed to spending what we earn because we are always trying to increase our standard of living, but there are many things we can sacrifice in the short term if we know we'll reap the rewards many times over in the long term. Again, it's just about focusing on those really important long-term goals and applying some persistence and determination.

With everything running smoothly and the properties going well, I now had the time to spend focusing on building my property business further, however I soon began to struggle to find the deals and actually got a bit stuck. I couldn't make sense of it, but the more I looked and the more time I spent analysing numbers and trying to improve them, the more I just couldn't find anything that worked for me. I was now a full-time investor so therefore I assumed that I would just get all these fantastic deals jumping out in front of me but it wasn't happening.

I soon realised what was going on: I was looking for 'the perfect deal'. These deals do come along, but they're very rare, and by just looking for the *perfect* deal I was missing out on some great opportunities that still delivered good numbers – I just hadn't been satisfied they were good enough for me. By putting myself under pressure to be truly excellent, I had forgotten the most important thing about being an investor: to keep buying. As long as the numbers work, keep going.

My investor from my 3rd property got the returns we had planned, so was happy to fund more deals. With investment lined up and my search criteria sorted out, I secured three more properties almost back to back. A bit like buses, they all came along at once and, while they may not have beaten some of my previous deals, they were still great deals. The projected cash flow figures would really begin to take me to the next level and a few more rungs up the ladder. I have always remembered what I learnt from that experience: the harder you look for the perfect deal, the less you will see. Keep yourself in the market, let people know what you are looking for and the deals will find you.

It would have been very easy at that point to think I had made it. I was working for myself, I owned a few properties and had more income than I had earned in full time employment, but I had also learnt about the power and value of deferred gratification. Most people in society want instant gratification and are not prepared to wait to spend money on what they want. How many times have we heard stories of people that have won the lottery, spent all the money immediately and shortly afterwards have nothing to show for it? If they had just saved or invested a small percentage of those winnings, they could have had a great time for the rest of their lives. Any money that I was making was going back into the properties and not being wasted on flashy items - some may call it being tight but I would call it being sensible. Yes, I celebrated my successes but I didn't let things go to my head, because I knew how much further I needed and wanted to go in order to realise my big goals. The real rewards would come if I kept my head down and just got on with things. Deferring the day when you get a payback on your achievements will make the payback even bigger when it actually comes.

The next stage for me was to really treat this as a business, look at my set-up and think about employing people to do some of the work for me. That was the logical next step and I found that taking the business to that next level had both good and bad aspects. Within a relatively short period of time, not only had I become self-employed, running a business, but I was now going to be managing members of staff as well. That new comfort zone I had grown into was going to be stretched again.

Chapter 4

Full time investor and business owner

At the start of my investing journey - when I was sat down with Steve, trying to work out what it was that I was going to do - I set myself the target that my property business should generate enough income that it would replace the salary from my full time job. Even though I had never really been sure I would actually get there, I now had and it felt great. I'll be honest, though; it also felt a little unusual, as I had never been self-employed before, and that was a big change.

I didn't have a boss telling me what to do, where to be and what time to be there. I didn't have work colleagues that I could speak to every day. I didn't have a daily routine set out for me. Don't get me wrong, I was glad to be out of that, but it meant the responsibility fell to me to plan my own days, make my own business contacts and then actually work when I felt it would be the most productive use of my time. That one factor – being able to work when you feel you can be most productive – can be a luxury, as long as you are disciplined. If you're a night owl, it can be great to have time off during the day and then work during the evening. Some people work best at 2 o'clock in the morning, and that's just not possible if you're in a job with office hours that demand you work 8am to 6pm.

The key is to find out how and when you work best and then plan your days accordingly.

Making sure you're working productively

How many times have you spoken to work colleagues or business contacts about their jobs and asked if they're busy? Why do we use 'busy' as a measure of success? The standard answer from most people is, of course they are busy, they have lots going on! Those who say they aren't busy are genuinely probably not and may be struggling with where they are at in life. There is, however, a big difference between being busy and being productive; knowing the value of your time and making the best use of it.

I would rather be busy for 4 hours a day and for those 4 hours to be the most productive they can be, than to be generally busy for 8 hours and probably only get half the work done. As employees, we are all judged to an extent by what time we turn up and what time we go home. Very rarely is there a measure of productivity built into that model – yes, there are targets and tasks to complete, but who is actually looking at whether everyone's making the best use of their time, rather than 'being busy for busy's sake'? It's a massive adjustment for most people when they step out of an employed position and suddenly realise that time really is money. As a self-employed person and business owner, my focus is now very much on productivity.

Being productive means you need to have a number of skills, the first of which is commitment. If you fully commit to each task you are doing then you can be very productive by prioritising your time and making sure the highest value tasks are completed first each day. Secondly, you need to be focused, and eliminate all the distractions around you that generally fill your days: phone calls, emails, surfing the internet, chatting with friends or work colleagues, watching TV, etc. And thirdly, you need discipline. You must take responsibility for planning your own schedule and sticking to it. (You may need to work with a business coach or mentor to help you, and I'll talk about that more in Chapter 8). Those three skills, combined, will make you very productive, and I've found that in property it means you can make great progress while others just seem to be drifting from one thing to another. Planning effectively and working productively means you can be out there finding the best deals or sorting out problems without letting them take over your whole schedule.

Understanding that it's a business

Being self-employed means that not only do you need to be skilled in your specialism and knowledgeable about the sector within which you operate, but you also need to be good at business in general. Take, for example, a plasterer who is employed on a big site by a main contractor, imagines how much money the contractor is making and decides he could do that for himself. So he decides to go self-employed. He's still a plasterer, but now also needs to be able to market himself so that he has enough clients. What does he know about marketing or advertising? He needs business cards, leaflets, sign writing done on his van, etc. Being self-employed there is suddenly no guaranteed income, no paid holidays or sick days, and you tend to need a pot of savings you can dip into, because going from employment to self-employment generally involves an initial drop in income. If our plasterer has a family to support, he may be in for a challenging time.

He needs to decide whether he's going to earn money as a sole trader or set up a business. He'll need to do his own tax returns at the end of each year. He may need to find some suppliers or buy new equipment and suddenly that dream of simply earning more money turns into a sequence of responsibilities, issues and challenges that need to be tackled. The reality of self-employment may now not seem so rosy.

In my situation, I had always been employed and so I really was stepping out into a new world. Logging all my personal expenses as well as keeping records of the income and expenses of the properties was starting to take a lot of time. I had the normal inflow and outflow of tenants as well as problems at some of the properties that needed dealing with. I was out looking for more deals and starting to become busier than I was when I was in employment, so decided it was time to find someone to help out with the workload.

One of my friends was looking for some part-time work and we spoke about her coming on board to help out with the lettings side of things. It was a fairly informal arrangement and, for a while, it helped me and helped her, but that set-up only lasted for about six months. Property lettings is a difficult thing to do on a part-time basis, because the nature of the work – taking phone calls, carrying out viewings, dealing with maintenance issues, etc. - means it's not something you can switch on and off at different times. I tend to say that lettings is a part-time activity, but a full-time responsibility. If you are managing the properties yourself, you will have tenant problems from time to time and they usually pop up when you least expect them, outside of 'normal' working hours. The responsibility for your portfolio is always yours, even if you do employ a property manager or letting agent, because it is ultimately your business and you have to take an interest in what is happening, not simply leave others to it. I'm not saying you need to get involved on a daily basis, but it should be a part of your thought process to check in regularly with the people who are working for you or with you, to see how things are going.

I had never employed someone before - even in the jobs I had previously done, I never had anyone working under me. It felt strange to have someone calling me their boss and asking me what should be done. As the first person I employed was a friend, it was all fairly relaxed, which probably helped me become used to being in charge and taking the lead. I had always been a follower in my employed days; now I was out at the front, moving the business forward, and it was starting to feel really good.

I have learnt that all property investment needs to be treated as a business. Even if you have just one property, you should see it as a little business in its own right. You need customers (tenants) to provide you with income (rent) and there will be expenditure (mortgage, maintenance, etc.) that should be less than the income you receive. One of the great things with property is that the business element can, from a financial point of view, look very small compared to potential increases in the value of property over the medium to long-term. If you run it properly, the business should help you focus on cash flow and making a profit from the income alone, and then any increase in capital values is a bonus rather than a necessity and the sole purpose of your business model. As we all know - particularly through 2007-2010 - property markets can go down as well as up!

By the end of 2007, we had about 35 tenants. As you can imagine, that was bringing in some good income, but also generating a fair amount of work, so when my first member of staff left in November of that year, I felt like the whole world had collapsed around me. I was back in the position of doing all the work myself and, even though all the income was mine again, I had all the workload and problems to sort out. It really made me begin to think about the different roles within my business and the set-up that I was going to need as the business continued to grow. Early in 2008, I employed a new member of staff to do some of the lettings and property management work, and my first member of staff then came back to work for me in an office-based, administrative role that was much more suited to her skill set, helping me out with a lot of the financial aspects of the business.

During 2007 I also became the first franchisee for Steve's company, Platinum Property Partners. It was then – and still is, as I write - the world's first property investment franchise, based around the buy to let model Steve had taught me. What

I had achieved in the previous couple of years helped them demonstrate that the model really worked and that it was a proven, replicable & profitable system, which meant it qualified as a franchise. I had been relatively successful up to that point and yet I still hadn't ventured out into other areas of property investment, like international investing, commercial property, self build, development, etc., so I saw this business step as a great opportunity for me to grow, within the structure and framework of a franchise. I had already proved to myself and others that I could implement and develop a property investment strategy and that, with a little help and support, I could make a success of whatever I set my mind to. The idea of the franchise really appealed to me: it would help take me to the next level and also give me an opportunity to be involved in - and move forward with - a group of like-minded individuals from all over the UK, who would effectively become my business colleagues.

In my personal life, I had finally bought a house with my girlfriend and moved out of rented accommodation. You may think it a strange way to go, but I owned a number of investment properties whilst I was still living in rented accommodation myself, and that's just one example of the 'deferred gratification' I spoke about earlier in this book. Whatever money I was making in the early days was going back into the business, and in rented accommodation we could keep our living expenses low whilst the business was growing. The house that we bought in 2008 was much bigger, more expensive and nicer than we could have bought if I'd jumped in a few years earlier when I started investing in property, so it was well worth the wait. With the business growing, we also needed to have a dedicated office for me and the people that worked for me, so we converted the garage to provide the office space we needed. Suddenly the business really felt like a business, rather than just a hobby.

Systemising the business

Even with the property market going through a major correction, my business was really taking off during 2008 & 2009. We started managing HMO properties for other landlords, I was mentoring lots of other investors and showing them how to follow the same system I had, which was bringing in further income, and I was still buying more properties. This business was moving rapidly into the next stage, involving setting up and administering PAYE, dividends, salaries, corporation tax, office and public liability insurance; travelling around the country and staying away for a few days at a time; reporting back to landlords on how their properties were performing, etc. We needed to be systemised and improve as a business, particularly now that we were accountable to other investors as well. Within the framework of the franchise, there were many systems in place already, which I and my team were able to adapt and improve for our own circumstances. Many of those were then fed back into the franchise.

Systemisation is one of the biggest lessons I have learned about running a business. If you have good systems in place, it makes things so much easier, saving time, reducing duplication and helping to minimise errors. With correct systems in place you also reduce the risk to your business. If you think of all the different aspects involved in running a property portfolio, then you can appreciate it really does need some organising. Lettings, property management and maintenance, rent, mortgage, insurance, tax returns, paying bills, solicitors, mortgage brokers, furnishing...the list goes on and it's essential you have systems and procedures to deal with each of these elements.

Unfortunately, too many businesses rely on the knowledge of certain individuals to be able to operate, and if that individual leaves, the business begins to collapse. With correct systems, you have a structure that holds your business together, so that if someone leaves a certain role, you can replace that person with someone else relatively easily. Of course, there will need to be some transfer of knowledge and some training, but you certainly reduce the impact that the loss of a key member of staff can have. My goal here was to set up the business so that eventually it could operate with very little – or ideally none – of my involvement on a day-to-day basis, which would allow me to focus on other things, be that doing new deals, networking and learning, doing exercise or simply spending time with friends and family. That's still a goal I'm constantly working on, but I'm pleased to say I'm pretty much there now.

As my business has grown, we have changed our systems and set-up many times over, because in some ways I didn't look far enough ahead at the start. I had been putting systems in place that worked for the stage of the business we were at then, rather than really focusing on where we wanted to get to. I don't beat myself up about that, because it's difficult as a small business to invest in the future when the priority is today, and I've learned from everything I've done.

My recommended reading on this subject of transfer from employment to self-employment, and then business owner and systemisation, is a great book by Michael Gerber called *The E-Myth Revisited.* Whatever stage of business you are at, and whatever sector you operate in, I can guarantee you that you will be able to identify with what he says and recognise your own position regarding where you are now and where you may have been in the past. Please do go and buy yourself a copy.

At that point I realised I had become a full-time professional investor and it was a great feeling to be able to say to people that's what I was. A lot of people have the impression that professional investors swan around all day, either schmoozing or doing nothing, while things just happen, but the truth is, it's those who have worked really hard to get to that position and set up really excellent business models that make it seem effortless and are the biggest successes. I always smiled whenever people asked me what I did with my time - hopefully you now have an understanding of what I was working to achieve with my business and how much time, effort and organisation it took.

At the end of the day, no one will do that groundwork for you. The drive to make it happen and make your business a success has to come from within, and with the right goals in place to help keep you on track, and a great deal of persistence, determination and focus, it can be achieved. Make sure you have a big enough goal and a firm commitment to achieve it, and I promise you and your business will grow and improve massively.

Chapter 5

Learning to work within an ever-changing market

Those of you that have lived through and experienced previous housing market booms and busts will know that 2008 to 2011 has been a tricky ride for most property investors. Having started at the end of 2005 and become a full time investor by the start of 2007, I was lucky to have benefitted from ideal investing conditions, with ready availability of mortgage finance and a rapidly rising market. Property was the 'in' thing and almost everyone was jumping on the property investment bandwagon. But, for me, making money is not just about going along with the market. It's about out-performing the market, seeing angles that others can't and being able to take advantage of opportunities that others may see as threats. Those that have been truly successful, not just in property, but in any industry, are the ones that are able to see what the masses are doing and then do something completely different themselves.

As a first time buyer and property investment novice, I had no perspective of a market correction or when/if it might happen. Nevertheless, I understood the good sense in focusing on rental income and profit, and treating capital increases as a bonus. Two years after I bought my first property, it was valued at 20% more than I had paid for it and I hadn't spent anywhere near that much money on improvements. That seemed a crazy situation to be in, but one that I was fortunate to benefit from, although it did give me a skewed impression of the property market. With hindsight, making a substantial rental profit each month and having the value of the asset that I owned go up 20% in two years was clearly an unsustainable situation.

In a rising market, as it was then, actually buying property was difficult, as there was a lot of competition from other people who also wanted to buy a property that they knew would be worth more than they had paid for it almost instantly. At that time, if the period between agreeing to buy a property and completing on the purchase took a few months, you could actually make a few thousand pounds! It was also very easy for estate agents to make their money – properties were flying off the shelves - the difficult part of their jobs was having sufficient stock to sell. It was not uncommon to have sealed bids for 'bog standard' properties, gazumping was a fairly regular occurrence, and vendors knew they were in a position to demand a certain price, because so many people were trying to buy.

Many homeowners were seeing this rise in the value of their home and using that new equity to improve their standards of living. People were releasing equity to go on holidays, get new cars, buy new kitchens, etc. and generally living on their new-found wealth. They were essentially supplementing their income with the capital growth from their homes and getting used to a standard of living they couldn't really afford. It was not a sustainable way to live and, as we now know, the levels of personal debt in the UK rose to some staggering levels during this time. Some correctly predicted the end of that boom period, while some proudly suggested that the property market would continue to rise and, even though it had performed differently in the past, the future of the property market was only headed upwards.

As a novice investor, I didn't really know what to think - my major concern was making sure the rental income came in each month. I was happy to keep my head down and stick to the basics. I couldn't do anything about the market but I could control my own property, my tenants, my mortgage payments, etc. and so that, for me, was the most important thing. If the market went up, then great, but the most important thing was for me not to be majorly affected if it went down.

Throughout 2007, which was one of my most active buying years, the market continued to rise in the first half of the year, but then the second half began to show signs that the market was slowing. During that year, I was very much focused on my strategy of buying properties for income, therefore HMOs were the way to go. You could still refinance properties almost immediately after you had bought them, for a higher figure, and then any money you had put into the property would come back into your pocket. You simply swapped your cash for more debt. Mortgage rates for BTL (buy to let) deals were still around 5-6%, availability of mortgages was plentiful and there were many different lenders to choose from. My profit margin gave a very comfortable cushion against costs and / or interest rates rising and I was getting an excellent return on my capital invested.

2008 was really the year when the 'rules of the game' changed overnight, in terms of what I had known up to that point. News of the sub-prime mortgage market collapse in America really started to take hold and the knock-on effect of that was starting to bite in the UK. 2008 was the year that the term 'credit crunch' became familiar to everyone and suddenly the confidence of all those involved in the property market began to drain away. The media headlines predicted doom and gloom and told everyone that the property market was probably facing a downward turn, buyers stopped buying and so property prices started dropping. There were some that thought they would be okay and their property would not drop as much in value as others in the street or neighbourhood. But while it's true that some people have been affected more than others, absolutely everyone involved in the property market has experienced big changes.

The easy debt on which the property market had grown, up until 2008, suddenly tightened up. LTVs (Loan to Values) on BTL properties had reached a peak at 90% but then suddenly began to drop - first to 85%, then 80% and then 75%, which is the level they settled at for a couple of years. As I write, the BTL mortgage market seems to be improving, in terms of the number of products available and increases in LTVs to 80%. There is now one product at 85%, which has not been seen since 2008, and maybe that's a sign of confidence coming back into the market.

The availability of finance has always played a massive part in the growth and adjustment of the property market. From a borrower's point of view, I believe they were too frivolous with mortgages in the good times but then become too stringent in the tough times. I can understand the lenders not wanting to be too exposed to any possible further price falls, but we have probably all heard of decent people, with decent credit ratings and solid business models that have not been able to get mortgages, and that has not helped the market as a whole. If money is lent to the right people on the right properties, then the market will begin to move on again.

During this time of change, many investors were getting out of the market. With LTVs dropping, it meant that the days of investing in property without putting in any of your own money were over. Many amateur investors were flushed out of the market and it was left to the professionals to take the pick of the best deals. Having become comfortable being in the minority, I could see that it was a great time to buy property as, even though there were predictions of further falls in capital values, some people were so keen to get out of the market that they were prepared to sell their property at a significant discount. Not only were we looking at purchase prices below the peak values of 2007, but also well below the values they dropped to in 2008, 2009 and 2010. My 'best' deals were done during this time, as the difference between what the properties were valued at and what I paid for them were so large – usually around 30% - that any further falls would just eat into the in-built equity, rather than put me into the negative equity situation that many people find themselves in during a falling property market. I was still focused on rental profits and cash flow, but with the added bonus of in-built equity.

So the deals were there for the taking; the issue was the amount of capital required, which I'll talk about shortly. The investment model of buying a property, doing some work to it and then refinancing it shortly afterwards to get all your own money back out, was virtually gone overnight, because of the falling loan to values, flat or falling prices and a new FSA ruling that meant that you could not refinance a property until 6 months after you had taken ownership of it. The rules were changing all the time, mortgage products were disappearing almost daily and mortgage offers from lenders were being withdrawn without any notice. I had never experienced that sort of situation before but, rather than let it negatively affect me, I just kept my head down, focused on finding the best deals I could and got on with things. I couldn't affect any of those external factors, so I simply continued to find ways to make things work, rather than focus on how the market had been in the past and wondering when or if it might return, as too many people were doing. Those days of buying houses more-or-less for free and making easy money were gone, but there were still ways of moving forward for those with the commitment to find them.

You may have noticed that I haven't used the term 'market crash'. That's because it has been, in reality, simply a correction. The media have screamed 'crash' because they want to dramatise the situation to sell their papers or get more hits on their website – remember, the media is fundamentally about selling papers and advertising, and bad news always sells better than good. But common sense should be enough to tell you that property always has an intrinsic value – our population is increasing and people always need a roof over their heads – so, unlike shares, which can lose all of their value virtually overnight, property will hold that basic value of the bricks and mortar with which they are built.

The market correction was also very different, depending on where you were based in the UK and the type of property you had. I was only concerned with my local market and my local area, which, in general, survived the downturn fairly well. The fundamentals of the town are strong, with good local employment, a large commuter population and consistent, strong tenant demand. Prices do not rise massively but they don't fall massively either – it's a steady and reliable market. There is always talk of 'average' price rises or falls and, depending on who produces the report, you will often get very different figures on what is happening now and what has happened in the past. Don't worry about national averages, just focus on your specific properties, the areas they are in and how those are performing. Towns in other parts of the UK do not matter unless you have property there!

Earlier, I mentioned a book called *The Dip*, and here is another great case of that coming into play. The property market was taking a dip, mortgage lending was taking a dip, confidence was taking a dip but I was still able to buy more properties, find better opportunities and continue to grow my business. Having the ability to understand what was happening and, more importantly, see how I could benefit from it, really helped me to continue moving forwards. Many investors simply got stuck in that dip and have still not come out of it. They might, once the market begins to rise, but I wasn't prepared to wait. I worked hard to understand how I could buy properties in a falling or rising market and still make money, and that's what has made me a professional investor rather than just an amateur.

Those market conditions also really highlighted to me the benefits of the investment model I had been taught, which was to invest in property primarily for the cash flow. I saw many investors and developers go bust because their 'model' relied on the value of property rising. (How they could call capital appreciation a 'strategy' is still beyond me!) Once that stopped and finance became difficult to get, they had no other exit route and their business model was exposed as fundamentally flawed. It's very easy to think that the good times will continue forever, but if you look back at the property market over the last 50 years or so, you'll see it naturally works in cycles. The general trend has been for it to rise, but along the way there are many peaks and troughs. The basic principle of focusing on income means you can ride through the troughs and get a bonus when you are going up the peaks. You really can have your cake and eat it if you invest in the right properties and do it correctly.

All this isn't to say I haven't been affected by the property market corrections – I have. The value of some of the properties I own will have fallen, but that value is simply a number on paper to me, because I'm not intending to sell them any time in the foreseeable future. Why would I want to sell properties that are giving me a good income? I've mentioned it several times already, but the focus on income has protected me from the potential negative impact of falling values. As with any business, cash flow is king, and if there isn't enough cash coming in then the business will eventually die. With property, if you don't have enough money coming in to pay the mortgage and bills, eventually the mortgage company will want their money back and will repossess your home or investment property. The sexy part of property is the potential increase in value of a portfolio, but the lifeblood of it *must* be rental income.

Development is a completely different strategy, and one that was very badly affected during this time. The value of the vast majority of developments fell significantly because there were fewer buyers willing to hand over deposits for off-plan properties as LTVs for new-build flats dropped to 60%. And without an alternative exit route, some developments were completely mothballed or stopped mid-way because the money had run out, while others were simply sold at any price, just so the developers could get out before they made any further losses.

This 2-3 year period of change also emphasises another key point, which is that you should always view BTL property as a medium to long-term investment. The value of a portfolio today is nothing compared to the value it will have in 20-30 years' time. Along the way it will go up and down, but I'm looking at the capital value of my portfolio as my pension provision, and the monthly profit from it as my income in the meantime, until I reach that point in life where I want to realise some of its value. You can make and lose a lot of money by dipping in and out of a market over a short period of time, so, to eliminate those risks, you do need to put a longer-term perspective on any BTL investment that you make. Don't rely on it to make you a millionaire overnight! Small, steady increases in capital values alongside positive cash flow will, over time, make you wealthy.

Even more changes...

In the sector within which I was investing, there were many other changes, in addition to prices falling and mortgage finance availability tightening. HMO Licensing came into play in 2006 and really began to take effect in 2007; planning permission rules changed during both 2009 and 2010 (and that may change again in 2011); protection schemes for tenants' deposits were introduced in 2007, and it would have been very easy to be knocked over by all these changes. Many of them were making life and business much harder for landlords and investors, but I was in a network of like-minded individuals within the franchise. We regularly met and talked to each other about new ways of doing things, with the mindset, 'come on, if we can't do it, nobody can'! The importance and power of having a great support network around me really came into play during these times and it was also great to be able to help others. Property can be a lonely business, but if you can surround yourself with good people who understand what you are going through and can help you find solutions to challenges, that has enormous benefits.

It's impossible to talk about this period of time without also mentioning the dramatic reduction in the Bank of England Base Rate and the effect that has had on many investors. We currently have a base rate of 0.5%, which has resulted in many investors benefitting from massively reduced mortgage payments, and they may be sitting pretty thinking that they are in a good position. It may well be a good position, but it is a false one. When rates do increase – and with inflation figures rising, a base rate rise looks possible in the next few months - the profit they are making now could soon reduce to nothing. The average BTL yield is typically about 5% and that is the 'break even' position for many investors, with some having to subsidise their investment, even at that level. You can see that it wouldn't take much of a move in rates to eliminate any surplus cash they have been making in the last couple of years.

I benefitted myself from the reduced rates on many of my properties, but in recent times have been moving some of my mortgages on to fixed rate products, for two reasons. Firstly, the base rate is only going to go up and, secondly, I wanted to have a mixed bag of mortgages in the portfolio so I won't be fully exposed to a rate rise on all my properties. I have calculated the 'break even' point for my properties and, generally, it's at least double the average BTL rate, so I have some good insulation.

Of course, I hope that after a long period of low rates we don't have a long period of high rates...although high interest rates would present some great buying opportunities!! But whether clouds will come with silver linings, only time will tell.

Chapter 6

Sharing my knowledge

There is a saying, "Those who can, do; those that can't, teach." I couldn't disagree with that more. My success – and the fact that I even got started on my journey in the first place - was largely due to the fact that someone who had been successful themselves was able to teach and mentor me to follow their investment system. That one-to-one form of education and motivation has been proven, time and again, to be the best way to help people successfully put into action what they learn.

Mentoring is very different from coaching. To be a coach you don't necessarily have to have achieved yourself the things you are teaching people – it can merely be your 'specialist subject'. But to be a mentor you need to have been there, done it and got the t-shirt. Whether you are a coach or a mentor, you are asking people to follow a certain system or format; the difference is that mentoring is about actually bringing to life your own experiences, demonstrating how others can replicate your systems and successes and then supporting them through the process.

Having been mentored myself and achieved a certain level of success, in 2007 I was asked by Steve to mentor other first time investors who wanted to follow the same system I had been taught. This was another stage of being asked to step out of my comfort zone! It was all well and good doing my own investments and focusing purely on myself, but to be asked to help other people as well was quite a step up. When you do something every day, it becomes habit and feels relatively easy, and I had begun to do lots of things almost without thinking. To then be asked to explain why, how, when, what, etc. was initially very challenging. Added to that, I felt a great weight of responsibility to make sure that other investors didn't go wrong, that they were aware of all the different options available to them and they had enough information and support to be able to make the progress that they wanted.

The vast majority of people that I initially mentored have gone on to buy properties. Those that haven't were either not really in a position to be able to buy, or have gone on to do other investments outside of property, so I have no doubt that their mentoring experience will have helped them in one way or another.

It's very interesting to work on a one-to-one level with people from different backgrounds, with different levels of experience and different ways of learning. The more mentoring I did, the better I became at it, as I began to quickly understand what approach worked best and find ways to present the information I wanted to give them in a way that suited their learning style. Some people have been more visual learners, wanting to see me write everything down, draw diagrams or show them pictures, while others were happy simply to sit and listen and learn. Some people I've mentored have struggled with the numbers side of things and some have needed more help with understanding and navigating the rules and regulations for HMO investments. Some have only needed to hear things once and others have needed them repeating over and over again. But amongst all these different learning styles, the one thing I could always rely on was the proven system itself - the solid model I was teaching people for buying and renting out HMOs in the most profitable way possible.

One of the main tests of my mentoring ability was to be able to go to the town or city where the investor lived, and then help them find and negotiate on a property that would both fit the investment model we used and deliver the financial results that we expected. There were varying levels of support available afterwards, but those were the main criteria we needed to fulfil in the initial two days of mentoring. I have now mentored people in over 30 different towns and cities around the UK and some of those I have been back to several times. And while every town and city has a number of differing factors to consider, the particular HMO model I teach people has worked in every single one of them. The property prices and rental prices may vary, but it is very powerful to have a core system that works anywhere – you just need to help people understand how to apply it in their own investment location. I recently estimated that over all the mentoring days I've done with people, I've been in and viewed more than 1000 properties, so you might say I know a thing or two about the ones that work best for this strategy!

I have also developed a lot as an investor myself through mentoring others. Constantly having to think about what I'm doing and saying to others has really kept me sharp and focused on how I can improve what I do and how I do it. It's probably no coincidence that I bought most of my properties in 2007 and bought my best deals in 2008 & 2009 when I was doing more mentoring than ever before. And as I develop as an investor, I know I'm becoming more productive as a mentor, so my clients are increasingly getting a better and better service from me – mentoring really is a win-win.

In 2008 I was asked to step up to the next level and only mentor those people that joined the franchise. Most of these investors were older than me and had far more business experience, so I couldn't help but feel a little bit nervous at the thought of *me* being *their* mentor! What I had to keep reminding myself was that although they had good business skills, most of them had only ever bought their own home and had certainly never invested in property in the way that I was going to teach them.

One of my favourite mentoring experiences was with a guy called Philip, who had been the worldwide Finance Director for the Norwich Union/Aviva Group. He was older than me, had more business experience than me, more investment capital than I had to start with, and yet I was going to teach him all about investing in HMOs! We spent some time, on the phone and via email, short-listing properties that we thought would fit the criteria, before spending two days in his hometown of Norwich, viewing them to see which one would work best. One property that I remember short-listing had somehow dropped off the list of properties that Philip had arranged for us to view. I just knew that this property would be the perfect one for him to buy before we had even seen it. He, however, didn't like the look of it, so had not booked a viewing, but that soon changed when I got up to Norwich!

I think I was far more excited about the property than he was, but he couldn't argue with the potential that I pointed out and we ended up making an offer on the property, which was accepted. That property is now up and running and it's the biggest cash flowing property of any that I have found for people when I have been mentoring them in any town or city around the UK. It beats any of the properties that I own myself – it's something I could only dream of finding in my own town – and whenever I see Philip, I always remind him of the incredible cash machine he nearly missed out on! He has since gone on to buy a number of other properties himself, but helping get him and his property business off to such a strong start is something that I am very proud of.

I have also mentored a couple of brothers who have since gone on to buy numerous investment properties in different locations around the UK and now operate another property franchise business. It is great to know that I played a major part in their development and helped them start their own investment journeys in the way that was right for them.

And on three occasions now I have been out viewing properties with new mentees and, before we have had a chance to explain who we are, the agent has assumed we're Mum, Dad & son viewing a potential family home. I now have three unofficial sets of parents in the franchise world, which is absolutely fine by me, because the network really is like a family!

I genuinely enjoy and have a real passion for helping other investors and it's great to keep hearing about their successes, while being there to help them overcome the various hurdles and obstacles they meet along the way. To have the knowledge and experience to be able to answer pretty much any question they throw at you is very powerful and something I'm very proud of. That ability, combined with the success of my continuing investments, means I can honestly say I qualify as a professional investor in the world of HMO investing.

As well as broadening my experience of investing around the UK, mentoring and helping others has given me a number of more personal benefits. Seeing the successes of the people I have mentored has given me great pleasure and also more confidence, not just in me as an investor but also as a person in my daily life. And mentoring is another source of income that has helped me to grow my business. Having multiple streams of income is important, so that you are as insulated as possible against any potential recessions or problems in one area of your business. In my case, if my property rental income drops for any reason, then I have other sources of income that can cover that. Look at any successful businesspeople and you'll see that one of the things they have in common is either multiple businesses providing income, or multiple sources within one type of business.

Hopefully this chapter has already helped you understand some of the many benefits of mentoring, but I'd like to end by stressing just how much it can help you, personally and professionally. Paying for someone to mentor you on a one-to-one basis is usually a more expensive learning option, but I can almost guarantee that the value you receive will far outweigh that cost. It's a bit like having a personal trainer helping you at the gym, rather than just going there alone. It will cost you more but, in the vast majority of cases, the results you get with a personal trainer will be much better than anything you can achieve on your own. The thing you have to make sure you get right is your choice of mentor. If you think you've found someone suitable, 'interview' them to make sure they're not only going to be able to teach you what you want and need to learn, but also that they're a 'fit' for you, personality-wise. Ask them about their background and what they have achieved, and – particularly in the case of a constantly changing business market, like property – make sure they are still successful today and doing the type of investing that they are mentoring you in. I found the right mentor for me and it was life-changing.

Chapter 7

Growing my business

One of the main advantages of becoming a full time investor and being able to employ people to work for me, was that I could delegate most of the property management and administration, freeing myself up to focus on specific, high-value tasks. Rather than getting bogged down in day-to-day office work, I could use my time more productively, looking for more and better deals and developing and growing the business – spending more time working 'on' it, rather than 'in' it.

In any industry or market sector you hear stories about people who always seem to have opportunities appear in front of them and they're usually referred to as the 'lucky' ones who get all the great deals. But it's no fluke that this happens. Once people know that you're in the market for certain types of deals, your reputation grows and your name spreads so you become known as someone who will always be worth putting those deals in front of. So what is your niche? How would people in your industry know you or talk about you?

To get a good reputation, you need to be able to perform and be true to your word. If you tell people that you are a 'cash buyer' and can exchange contracts in 28 days, then you need to be confident that you can achieve that. There's nothing worse than getting a reputation as someone who talks a good game but, when it actually comes to the crunch, can't step up to the plate. And bad reputations spread much faster than good ones. Estate agents like to know that they have a small group of investors they can rely on, so that when the right deal comes along, they can make a few phone calls and 'in principle' get the deal done.

I have always been very specific with estate agents about the types of properties I'm interested in. Right from the start of my investment journey, I was very clear about my requirements for properties which could be rented out on a multi-let basis and gave them some specifics of my search criteria. You might think that being very specific will mean you miss out on certain deals, but I have always found the reverse to be true - that by being specific, you can almost guarantee the agent will call you first if that type of property comes up. If you go into an estate agency and simply tell them you are looking for 'investment property', can you imagine how many other people will be included on that long list? In fact, you may not even *make* their list because they will have heard that phrase so many times before. You need to make yourself stand out and become the 'go to' person in your town or area for certain types of properties and deals.

My expertise in the world of HMOs has allowed me to develop good, mutually beneficial relationships with estate agents, surveyors and other landlords in the same sector or other areas of property investment. I have often had surveyors asking me how these kinds of properties work, what sort of tenants I have, where I advertise, etc. - it seems as though there are still not very many people specialising in this form of investment and not many actually treating or running it as a proper business. Working in what seemed to be very much a niche area of the buy to let market, and approaching my strategy and contacts in the right, professional way, I was able to put myself in the 'deal flow'. Once I had a small portfolio behind me, I found I was able to grow it relatively quickly as certain deals begun to find me, rather than me having to go looking for them.

When the deals started to find me...

With the third investment property that I purchased, the retired neighbours took a keen interest in what I was doing with the house. They wanted to see the different stages of refurbishment and find out what we did, in terms of how we rented the property out, and who would be living there. I could have taken the stance of being fairly guarded and trying to keep them at arm's length, but there appeared no harm in keeping them involved and up to date with the progress we were making. Initially, they were a little frosty about my plans for renting it out on a room-by-room basis but, once they saw the standard of the property and knew that I had others properties in the area already up and running, their initial concerns faded and we started to build up a good relationship.

On one occasion I arrived at the property to check on the progress of the refurbishment and the neighbours were outside their property. The man began to explain that they planned to move to Norfolk in the next 6 months and would be looking at selling their property. They asked if I would be interested in buying it and (of course) my response was that I would be, and that we should discuss the plans further. It was still some way off, but they knew that I was keen to buy more property in that area, their property was exactly the same as the one I had bought already, and if they could avoid going through an estate agent they would save themselves some money.

A few months later, they said that their plans were now definite and that they wanted to see if we could agree a price. Within about 15 minutes we agreed a deal, on the same terms as the house that I had already purchased, and everyone was happy. The couple got a buyer they knew, liked and could trust, and I got a property that fitted my investment criteria and would be easy to manage as it was next door to another of my properties. It was a perfect win-win. I had never thought before about approaching any neighbours to see if they would be willing to sell but, simply by being in a position to be able to let the deals find me, I had bought another great house. I also then spoke to the neighbour of *that* property, which was very run down and looked like it needed some investment. Although we came close to doing a deal, it didn't actually work out, but I would probably have tried going all the way up the street if I had got that third one as well! It just shows that there are deals to be done everywhere and, as long as people know you are in the market for them, they will often find you.

Another great example of this was an estate agent that I had only actually bought one property through, but that I had developed a good relationship with because I had stayed in regular contact. They made me aware at a very early stage of some properties that they were likely to be instructed on, because they thought the properties fitted my criteria exactly. It was about 9 months between them giving me this 'heads up' and the properties actually coming to the market, but they had lined me up as the first person to view them. The properties were ideal and, after some negotiation, I agreed the purchase of two of them - which have turned out to be great investments. I didn't know these properties existed, who owned them, or that they would be coming on to the market but, by having the right contacts and being specific about my criteria, I was able to get in first, negotiate a great deal and we all got something out of it. The vendor 'sold' two properties pretty much before they were officially available, the agent would get his commission relatively quickly and I got two great investment properties to add to the portfolio. I have no doubt that more deals will find me through those agents again in the future as a result.

Another interesting deal that I did was for a property in Chelmsford that was on the open market with a local estate agent. My initial feeling was that it was overpriced and this was actually confirmed by the estate agent, who said that they felt it should be a little cheaper but that the vendor was keen to test the market at that inflated price. It's always a good idea to ask estate agents how the property has been valued and whether the asking price they have is their valuation or that of the vendor, because, in some cases, those numbers can be very different. The agent is bound to act in the vendor's best interest, but when the price really is too high, you'll often find they're prepared to give you a hint of that, if they feel it really is in the vendor's best interest to get a quick sale to a committed buyer. In this case, it was on the market at £240,000 and yet the estate agent felt that £215,000 was a more realistic value. I initially offered £200,000, which was rejected outright by the owner, so a few days later I increased my offer to £205,000. After another few days, that offer was also rejected, at which point I then increased my offer to £210,000 and indicated to the agent that I would be highly unlikely to go any higher, considering their assessment of the value of the property and my own knowledge of the local market. £210,000 was rejected within hours. I seemed to be wasting my time with that one and was prepared to walk away, knowing that it's often those that are prepared to walk away that get the best deals.

After about two weeks, during which I had neither heard anything from the estate agents nor contacted them myself to find out if there had been any developments, I received a phone call from the agent, asking if I was still interested in the property. I said I was, and wondered what the reason was for the call - maybe the vendor had reduced the asking price? I was a bit shocked when the agent asked if I wanted to buy the property for £205,000. This took me back a little bit – you don't often get offered a property for £5,000 less than you've offered for it – so I asked for a bit of time to consider the deal. I phoned a couple of fellow investors to ask them their thoughts on what I should do, as I was a bit confused and sceptical about the sudden drop in price. Both people I spoke to said that sometimes deals are just there to be done. They both told me not to haggle over the price, simply accept that the deal had found me and not to worry or think about it too much.

Ultimately they were right, the deal was done and it has proved to be a great property. It has the highest occupancy rate of any of the properties in the portfolio and increased in value a lot through the refurbishment work that we did to it. Overall, that's another example of being in the right place at the right time and having the right reputation.

I often considered why it was that I was buying these properties and other people weren't and came to the conclusion that it was down to me having put myself into a niche position. Most of the properties I bought needed some form of refurbishment work and therefore would not be suitable for most families to move into, so that ruled out those buyers. The properties also tended to be larger 3 or 4 bed houses, so conventional buy to let investors, renting out on single tenancy agreements, would generally not be interested in them because of the low yield. With the work that needed doing as well, and the additional capital input required, the return would be even lower. Developers wouldn't be interested because, even though the properties needed some work, there wouldn't be a big enough margin to make it worthwhile for them so, again, I wasn't competing with those buyers. It left me virtually alone in a little niche, which I was able to exploit. And while it was great for me, it was also good for the agents because they knew that if the property wasn't suitable for the majority of their clients, then they had someone who could fill that gap, as long as the property was the right price and had the right layout potential to give the maximum number of lettable rooms.

Not only was I developing a good reputation with agents and surveyors in my local area, but I was also building a very good reputation within the franchise and soon became more of an expert on the day-to-day operating of these types of property portfolios than the owners of the franchise themselves. I was - and am still - used as one of their main case studies, as someone who has built a solid, sustainable property portfolio with a highly cash positive income. I stuck to their core model for buy to let investing and made a great success of it.

Diversifying the portfolio

During 2008 and 2009 I also started to grow the business and diversify the portfolio by purchasing properties at below their surveyed value (BSV). Most investors tend to use the term 'BMV', which stands for Below Market Value, but 'market value' means different things to different people and so that's a pretty fuzzy term. The value a surveyor puts on a property is not up for debate – it's a clear, legally supported valuation – and you should make sure, as I do, that every property you are buying BSV has been valued by an independent RICS (Royal Institution of Chartered Surveyors) surveyor. Different surveyors might give you slightly different figures – they do have a 10% leeway - but this is a valuation that mortgage lenders accept for mortgage purposes and therefore it's the most watertight assurance you can get that a property is worth what you think it is. And, ultimately, as a professional investor, you should be pretty sure yourself what a property is worth, before you instruct a surveyor.

I began to advertise in local newspapers and on the internet to let people know I was in the market to buy property and that I might be able to help solve their financial problems through the purchase of their property. This approach often takes a bit of time to generate interest and, initially, it didn't lead to many enquiries. But I pressed on and eventually agreed a deal with a couple who were getting close to being repossessed. They had been a two-income family but the wife had become ill and couldn't work, their income had dropped significantly, they were unable to keep up with all their bills and the mortgage payment was one of the bills that got missed. They had received a letter informing them of the date on which they would be required to go to court, at which point repossession proceedings would begin. That was when they realised how serious their situation was and knew they needed to do something about it, quickly.

The couple saw my advertisement in the newspaper and called to ask if I would be interested in buying their property. I took some details, went to see them the following day and within 24 hours we had agreed a price which would allow them pay off their mortgage and all the arrears, plus give them a lump sum of money to be able to do with what they wanted. One of the conditions of the deal was that they would to be able to stay in the property and live rent free for a period of time, to allow them to get themselves back on their feet. (This type of deal is no longer allowed as you need to be regulated by the FSA (Financial Services Authority) to do 'Sale & Rent Back' deals, but this deal was before those regulations existed.) I was able to buy the property at a substantial discount because the vendor was more driven by a pressing timescale to find a buyer than by getting full market value.

Again, I had put myself in a position where deals were finding me because I could do what I said I could and, again, both parties were happy with the outcome. The vendors had a buyer that they could trust, the repossession proceedings were stopped and they could continue with their lives. If they had been repossessed they would have had the embarrassment of being kicked out of their home, their credit rating would have been trashed and their children would have had to move schools if they had been re-housed in a different area. Instead, it was a win-win. In the 12 months following the sale, the wife got better and was able to work again, and the couple continue to be my tenants to this day.

I'm fully aware that some people take issue with this kind of investment purchase, because they see it as taking advantage of someone's misfortune and 'cheating' them out of the full value of their property. But being able to secure good property deals doesn't mean that you have to do it at the expense of other people. As long as you act with integrity and make sure that both parties are happy with the deal, you can all achieve your goals and benefit from it. When someone desperately needs to sell and there is nobody willing to buy their property at anywhere close to the asking price, investors like me are usually a very attractive alternative to repossession. We offer a solution that makes good business sense for us and also resolves the vendor's most pressing problems. Yes, there are some unscrupulous people out there, but I and all those within the franchise network always make sure that we leave these 'distressed sellers' in a much better position than we found them.

Buying property BSV is not normally a great cash flow strategy; it's more about turning cash into equity in property and being able to recycle any invested funds back out after a short period of time. BSVs are almost the opposite to HMO properties, which usually require more capital investment but also generate a higher return and more cash flow. While BSV properties might be more or less cash flow neutral, the benefit is that you are essentially buying equity in the property from day one, rather than having to wait and watch the property market go up, and are pretty much insulated against any market correction.

Obviously, the level of inbuilt equity is reliant on your ability to buy below the *true* market value, and you must make sure you've established that it's *today's* value. In 2008, 2009 and 2010, the property market in general was either flat or going down. A number of people needing to sell during this time had bought at or near to the peak of the market, which was probably back in 2007, so their own valuation of their property tended to be higher than its true market value at the time of selling. In a flat or falling market there are often great opportunities to find motivated sellers and get great deals, but it's a real test of your skills as a communicator. People don't actually want to sell their property at 25% or more below the surveyed value, especially when that surveyed value may be less than the price they paid for it! And I certainly went through yet another phase of expanding my comfort zone when I started looking for BSV deals.

I often hear other investors talk about 'negotiating' deals to buy property below market value, but you can't simply talk someone into selling their property for 25% below the value that a surveyor puts on it. There are no secret 'Jedi mind tricks' involved and no negotiation 'techniques' you need to go on courses to learn – you just need to understand the main factor behind the vendor's decision to sell the property and address it. The owners might be getting divorced or separating; a family member might have gone into care or died and they need money to pay for the health care bills or tax payments; the owners might have to relocate to another part of the country for work, etc. Ultimately, the strength of someone's desire to compromise on the value of their property, in return for the certainty of a sale and changing the equity in the property to cash in their pocket, will determine how motivated they are to sell at a lower price.

The best BSV deals I did were those that I was prepared to walk away from. You need to be very clear in your mind about the price that works for you and remember that you are not under any time pressure to compromise on that offer price. As I've already said, your motivation needs to be based on finding a solution that works for *both* parties, so understand the vendor's problem, offer a reasoned solution and put the ball back in their court, then be patient.

You can always negotiate the finer details of a deal and that doesn't always mean the price. The terms of the deal can be even more important for some people. Some vendors want to be given time to find somewhere to move to; some want a buyer that will fit in with their neighbours they are leaving behind; some want a buyer who will pay the estate agent's fees for them; some need their buyer to be able to move things along very quickly, etc. Knowing how to communicate and negotiate effectively in these often very stressful situations is vital, and your level of expertise can be the difference between winning and losing deals.

I think I did my best deals between 2008 and 2010, when the market was falling, and the two very best deals were never actually on the open market, meaning that I didn't have any competition for the properties – and that's the ideal situation to be in. Advertising, word of mouth and reputation all played their part in having these deals find me.

The best deals never reach the estate agent's window. That's not to say that agents are keeping them for themselves or doing anything underhand, but they will usually start their marketing by presenting properties to the people who they know will complete on deals. That means the vendor gets a solid buyer and the agent has the best chance of getting their commission quickly – as with any business, estate agencies run on getting their invoices paid! Agents often go to the same people; the ones that perform and who are in the deal flow. So understand that you will never get all the good deals simply by looking on the internet now and again. You need to build up your network of contacts, build your relationships with them and be willing to help others also, because when there are good property deals to be had, they need to be win-win for all parties involved.

How much does size matter?

When I first started investing in property I heard a number of people say that it becomes a bit addictive and now I can see why. When you own one property, you think that owning two would sound much better, and so on. Now, if you continue with that, it can become a never-ending game to acquire more and more properties, especially because investors are often judged by others in terms of how many properties they own. There are examples of investors that have hundreds of properties and got to the point where they have forgotten exactly what they own and even where the properties are! That just seems crazy to me. Yes, it's great to own lots of property, but you do need to be clear about your goals and objectives.

A portfolio with a hundred or so properties will require a lot of managing if you want it to perform as well as it can, and there are a huge number of investors out there with properties that are simply not very profitable because they're not being let and managed in the right way. And when the market is flat or falling, there's really very little benefit in having all those properties – they're more of a worry than anything else, as everyone waits for prices to recover. A smaller, well run portfolio can give you all you need – and actually be more profitable than a larger one - and so, for me, rather than the number of properties being important I want to know how those properties are performing, in terms of the monthly or annual cash flow or profit. I want to know the occupancy levels across the portfolio, the average yield and the return on investment of the capital in the properties. A small portfolio with high performance figures will require less management and be far less hassle than a large, poorly performing portfolio, so don't simply focus on the number of properties someone owns, because it can give you a misleading impression of them as an investor!

In the days of easy finance you could build a portfolio without investing any of your own cash and too many people were so focused on accumulating more and more properties, they forgot about the importance of making those properties perform as well as possible. When mortgage rates changed and/or mortgage payments were missed because these sloppy investors didn't have a sound business model behind their investments, the banks soon came calling for their money.

As I have grown my portfolio I have mainly used other people's money to finance the purchase and refurbishment costs. In the early days, it was relatively simple to recycle most - if not all - of the capital invested within a few months and that capital could then be rolled forwards into the next deal. With the drop in LTVs and prices stagnating or falling, together with the FSA's new regulations around refinancing, recycling capital became more and more difficult. It was vital that I adapted to the new market conditions if I wanted to keep growing the business, and this is when I started investing in BSV properties. As I was buying with inbuilt equity, it became easier to refinance those properties after an initial 6 month period had passed and get the capital invested back out. The amount of capital I was able to release depended on the revaluation of the properties – something that's always hard to gauge in a falling market - but this strategy allowed me to continue to grow the portfolio.

I was also able to reinvest some of the profit that I was making from the rental income into financing further purchases. This is obviously a slower strategy, as it takes quite a while for rental profits to build up enough to buy another house, but it can be done and is a legitimate and safe way of growing a portfolio. Everyone has a limited amount of capital and in property investment it's about recycling it to make that pot of money go as far as possible.

As and when market prices rise and loan to values increase, it will present me with further opportunities to grow the portfolio, if I so wish. But, as I've already said, it's not all about further growth. Some investors don't want a massive portfolio and so, over a period of time, they will probably pay down the amount of debt they have on the portfolio and increase the amount of equity. It's a very attractive feature of property as an investment that each investor can set their own goals and targets and there's such flexibility in terms of risk and debt. For now, I am definitely still in the growth phase and so am continuing to look for more deals all the time, leveraging as much of other people's money as I can.

Finally leaving home

I talked previously about the change from being in employment and starting my property portfolio, to going into self-employment and then becoming a business owner. The final phase of it really becoming a 'proper' business happened when I eventually moved the operation away from my house. Up until that point it had been a 'working from home' set-up and felt quite small-scale. But with multiple properties, multiple tenants and more staff it was, without doubt, very much a real business that I was continuing to expand. Not really knowing anything about commercial property as an investment, I began to look locally for some office premises to rent. One day I fully intend to buy an office property for the business and combine that with a residential investment, but that is a goal for the future.

The physical move into office premises really helped the business to develop. It made me look at it even more as a business and at myself not just as a property investor and owner, but as a businessman. We had started managing property for other investors; we agreed to sub-let part of the new office space to cover the overheads; we were having more and more tenants wanting to sign their contracts in the office and pay us rent or deposits in cash, and it made sense for the team that worked with me to be in more of a business/office environment. I had to become more focused on costs and income, setting budgets for the business, having monthly management accounts, etc. I am a property investor but I am also a property business owner and, as the business element has come into play more and more, I have become more successful. One of the reasons why we developed other income streams was to give us income that would not be affected by any possible interest rate rises. Income from managing other investors' properties, income from the sub-let of the office and income from mentoring other people were all things that I could control – it was 'safe' income that fitted in nicely, alongside the income from my own portfolio, with the development of the business.

When the business was based at home, it was all too easy to spend the whole day – and a lot of the evening - in the office, rather than be able to go home and get away from it. At times, that worked really well and I was able to put in the time necessary to develop the business but at other times it was difficult to switch off. I was fairly disciplined and, as my 'work' never really felt like work, it was easy to spend many hours just getting on with all the stuff that needed doing. When we moved the business out and into proper offices, I became more productive, because I would make sure that any time spent at the office was useful time. If I wasn't being productive, then it wasn't worth being there. It was nice to have a clear division between home and business and, even though I often work on a laptop, I can clearly switch on and off when needed, either at home or in the office.

I have since gone full circle and now, more often than not, work from home rather than in the office, as that leaves the team to get on with things without me bothering them! Obviously, I call in from time to time to make sure everything's okay, and there are still occasions where I need to work in the office, as that's where all the paperwork is held. But having the flexibility to choose where to work is great - such a difference to my days of employment when I had to be at my desk at a certain time in the morning and stay there until a certain time in the evening. Do I miss those days? I'm sure you can guess the answer to that one!

We now have the infrastructure in place to allow the business to develop and to put more properties into the portfolio. As that has grown over the years, I have adopted different structures and ways of working and that has been a gradual process, but I have learnt a lot along the way, learnt from my mistakes and now have a business that operates pretty much without me. Having a great team of people is vital to the success of the business and the portfolio. Never forget that you cannot be successful in property without good people around you.

Chapter 8

Developing myself

Over the last 5 years, I have developed even more as a person than as a property investor. The success of my business and my property investments is a direct result of me having developed as a person and as a business man. In any small business, the skills of the owner usually dictate the success (or not) of the business, and one of the key benefits for me of the journey I have been on has been the introduction to the world of personal development.

When I first heard about personal development, I had the impression of lots of 'happy clappy' people, asking me to close my eyes and 'visualise', while chanting silly mantras. There are plenty of people that subscribe to that kind of thing, but I wanted and needed more practical, down to earth support and development. Luckily, I have been introduced to some great people working in the field and have learnt a lot from them along the way.

I have always been a fairly shy and quiet person and, as a 26 year-old employee, embarking on a new direction in life, I had little confidence. I always preferred to keep my head down, get on with things and not focus too much on future plans and goals. I was simply rolling along with no clear direction. Life was just life and what would be, would be.

After finishing university in 2001, I was more than happy to put down the books because I'd never really taken that much interest in, or got much value from reading. But with my business studies degree and a love of most sports, I began to read autobiographies of some famous sportspeople, such as Jimmy Greaves, Lance Armstrong, Paul Gascoigne and Clive Woodward. I loved reading about their successes and challenges and how they had made their way to key points in their lives. There was not a lot to learn about business in these books, but in understanding the subjects more as people, I began to recognise some common traits.

Whilst they all had some natural talent and flair, they were all also prepared and keen to learn from others that had been successful, and would surround themselves with the best people in their industry. They would always strive to reach the next target or goal and always try to be the best they could. They had confidence in who they were and what they were trying to achieve and, particularly in the case of Lance Armstrong, developed an overwhelming desire and a determination to beat the odds to go on to become a great champion.

I still enjoy reading autobiographies about sportspeople, but, as I got closer to embarking on my property business and with encouragement from Steve, I also began to read the autobiographies of the 'celebrity' businesspeople that we all see on the TV - Richard Branson, Lord Sugar, Duncan Bannatyne, James Caan, Theo Paphitis, etc. There is a massive amount to learn in these books about how they have achieved their successes and the journeys they have gone through. Even though they operate in a different industry to me, there is still so much to learn, as many of the principles of success are the same, whatever industry you work in. There is a great saying - 'success leaves clues' - and you can find out so much by reading about what others have done. Why try and make it up for yourself when someone has already done it and written down their learnings for you?

As I started to become serious about property and the idea of building a portfolio that would give me income, I came across *Rich Dad, Poor Dad* by Robert Kiyosaki. Reading that book was a real 'lightbulb' moment for me. The good sense in acquiring assets that will generate income and minimise liabilities and expenses sounds very obvious on paper, but that book really bought the concept to life. I suddenly understood how the debt I would be taking on to buy them was actually 'good debt' because it was paying for an asset that would go up in value in the medium to long term and would generate an income in the meantime, which would more than service the debt. It was genuinely really interesting understanding how the 'rich' looked at money and used various fundamental principles to increase their wealth through the acquisition of assets, and I learnt a lot about the value of money. If you haven't already read *Rich Dad, Poor Dad,* make sure it's the next book you buy.

I do find myself going through stages where I will be really into books and other times when it couldn't be further from my mind, but I am currently reading about 10 books a year. If you don't read at all, just set yourself the target of one or two books a year. When you go on holiday and if you're travelling on the train, take a book with you and use the time when you may not be doing anything else to educate yourself a bit more.

Another great way of learning from successful people is to go and watch them speak at events or give seminars. I have been fortunate to hear people like Richard Branson (Virgin), Simon Woodroffe (YO! Sushi), Richard Reed (Innocent Drinks) and Mike Harris (Egg & First Direct) talk about their businesses, their plans and their biggest challenges, and I promise it's worth making the effort to get their top tips for success from them, in person. You usually have to pay to attend specific events where the best businesspeople are speaking, but you'll also find some of them giving free seminars at national exhibitions, so keep an eye out. If you can't learn from these people about business, then who can you learn from?

Setting goals

It's important to be learning from those that are already out there achieving their goals. Reading books, listening to audio programmes & watching key note speakers are all great ways to continually educate yourself and, once you start on that journey, you realise it is never-ending. There is always more to learn and there are always people that know more than you. If you approach things with that open-minded attitude, you will take on board so much more information.

I have found massive value in listening to some of the leaders in the field of personal and business development, such as Brian Tracy & Stephen Covey. Both are best-selling authors and real 'thought leaders' in their sectors. Brian Tracy's book called *Goals*, together with a talk of his I attended, really helped me see the value in setting goals and using them to lay out a plan for myself, rather than continue with the 'what will be, will be' philosophy that I once had. Having goals helps you to focus on what you really want to achieve in the coming months and have some clarity about what it is that you ultimately want to achieve.

I now set goals annually. I know some people that can set goals for the next 5 years, 10 years and even 20 years, but I really struggle to be able to set goals for longer than a 12 month period. I tend to use one of Brian Tracy's formulas, where I categorise the various areas of my life into: Personal, Education, Family, Health & Fitness, Social, Finance & Assets and Business & Charity. (Brian also has a category for Faith & Religion.) I have chosen to adapt his categories to my own circumstances - you need to find out what works for you and then put it into practice. I set my goals for the upcoming year and then regularly review them and adapt them. Depending on how detailed you want to get, those annual goals can be broken down into monthly or quarterly goals and you can then put together an action plan of how you are going to achieve them. The power of writing something down and not only mentally being aware of it, but also seeing it in black and white really does help to bring it to life. Goals need to be realistic, but don't be afraid to think big! Getting into the habit of setting goals and then achieving them is very rewarding, so if it's something you have never tried before, give it a go.

As a by-product of setting goals, I have now also become a 'list' person. The simple job of writing down a list of things to do is very, very basic, but so few of us do it. It's an interesting thought that people will write a list of the things they want to buy from a shop but don't write down a list of the things they want from life!! Try to get into the habit of sitting down at the end of every day, before you go to bed, and writing down a list of the things you need to do the next day. It will help you get things out of your head so you can sleep easy and means that when you wake up the next morning, you can get stuck straight into work and business, rather than getting up, planning the day, having a coffee and *then* getting started.

I love the saying, 'when the sun comes up, successful people are out running'. It doesn't literally mean that successful people are necessarily out getting in their physical exercise (although successful people do tend to be physically fit) but that as soon as the day starts, they are up and about, making the most of the time they have. We all have 24 hours in a day and yet some people are able to get more done than others. That's because they're organised, focused, energised and committed to being productive within the time they have. I wouldn't profess to being like that every single day, but I do try to be as productive as possible, rather than just busy, and having lists and goals enables me to do that.

My mentor, Steve, also introduced me to the concept of a vision board. This is a visual document that you create with images of things that you want in your life: a certain car, holiday destination, dream home, picture of a '6-pack' (not the beer variety!), a person that you want to meet, an activity that you want to be able to do regularly, etc. – any goal that can be visually represented. Find pictures from magazines or the internet, stick them on a large piece of paper and then put it on display in a place where you'll see it every day. The more you look at those images, the more likely they are to become absorbed into your subconscious and, over a period of time, the more likely they are to become a reality, as you subconsciously work towards making them come to life.

When I first heard this, I was convinced it fell into the 'happy clappy' side of personal development, but it really has worked for me over the years. I'm not saying that *everything* has come to fruition (not yet, anyway!), but I have got the car now that I wanted, I've been on some amazing holidays and I have a watch that looks exactly like the one on my vision board. You may say that's all just down to hard work, but I know that having those things on my vision board helped keep me motivated when times were tough and everything that's on there now is a constant reminder of the things I can have if I keep working hard. It's incredibly motivating when you can actually see some of the reasons why you want to be successful and the rewards that you can give yourself as you move towards your larger and longer-term goals. I can only endorse the use of goal setting and vision boards and know that they have played a big part in my personal development and journey.

The importance of surrounding yourself with the right people

There are two P's in the word property. The first P stands for Property itself, but the second P stands for People. You simply cannot be successful in property without good people around you and in order to develop the right contacts, you need to network. Now, networking events can be really hit and miss, so you need to be very clear about your objectives so that you can get as much out of the events as possible. To get the most out, though, you do need to put a lot in, and it can take a long time before you get any real value from networking, plus there are always people who just want to sell their wares that you have to make an effort to avoid. I've spent a lot of time over the years going to various property and business networking events and now prefer to network online, developing contacts, friends and followers on sites such as Twitter and LinkedIn. The benefit of doing it this way is you can be more specific about the people that you take the time to physically network with and turn only the best of these online contacts into real life contacts, cementing the relationship and gaining access to their wider network.

The strength of your network will have a strong influence on your overall success. If you spend more of your time with successful people and those that are leading their field, you are more likely to progress with them, rather than be left behind. Make sure you spend your valuable time networking with those that can help you and those that you can help also – as they say, always have one hand reaching up for help and one hand reaching down to help others.

Developing my business

Having never started or run a business before, I knew that at some point I would need to learn from others how to do that as well. In mid-2008, the business began to go through various changes that I realised I would benefit from speaking to someone about, so I started working with a business coach that had been recommended to me. A business coach won't necessarily give you all the answers, but they know the right questions to ask you, to make sure you understand why you do certain things and to challenge the decisions that you make. In essence, they like to play devil's advocate and get you thinking a lot more. I found this very useful as I was fairly naïve about business in general and there was huge benefit in talking things through with someone who was not only more experienced than me but who could also take an outsider's look at my business. It's all too easy to get bogged down in the day-to-day activities of the business and miss certain things, and it's amazing what a fresh pair of eyes can pick up.

Getting outside help is not always free and to get the best, most valuable help and advice, you will need to pay. But, as with mentoring, that investment in my business paid me back many, many times over. There are thousands of business coaches in the world and you need to find one that you get along with and that you know will be there to support you in developing your business. They won't do the work for you, but can be really instrumental in helping you become a better business person.

Building on both business coaching and developing my network of contacts, I helped establish a small 'mastermind' group. We meet on a regular basis to share our ideas, thoughts, successes and challenges and help each other to develop as people and business owners. Surrounding yourself with other successful individuals and people that you really get along with and respect is truly inspiring, and a group of like-minded people with a common goal is very powerful thing to be involved in. I always feel re-energised after spending time with people that are making progress and achieving some fantastic results. Sharing your goals, targets and plans with people in that kind of environment is also a really good way of making yourself accountable to others, because you know they'll keep asking you how you are getting on with achieving them. Between my mastermind group and my business coach, I know there's no chance of me slacking! It's a bit like having a stick to beat yourself with, but a very good one, that ultimately helps keep you focused and taking action.

You get back what you give out

Much of the journey about me developing as a person has been about my mindset and the way I am able to look at things and see them differently to the majority of people. Problems always used to be problems; now problems are opportunities to make improvements and just things that need to be worked out. Problems don't take over my life, as I have bigger goals to focus on and have my business coach, mentor, mastermind group and fellow franchise partners – not forgetting my vision board! – as constant reminders of why I do the things I do. I'm not saying that things don't get me down or cause me frustration, but I try not to let those issues get bigger than they really are, in the grand scheme of things.

I have recognised where my strengths are and where they are not and can see the positive aspects in most things. Being around negative people used to be comforting to me, because they would talk about their problems, which were often similar to mine, so I felt in good company, but now I cannot stand to be around negative people - they just drain the energy out of me. Talking about negative things only attracts other negative people and more negative situations. Talking positively about what you do and where you are going is much more enjoyable and it will make other positive people want to be around you.

There are many laws in this world but the Law of Attraction is one of the most powerful things you can use. You attract people, circumstances and opportunities into your life the more you think about and focus on them – much like how having a vision board works. Have you noticed how people who are on a downer just seem to attract more bad luck or more bad news? In contrast, it's been proven time and again that you attract better things simply by thinking in a more positive light, and I know that's been true for me. When you meet people and ask them how they are doing, most people have a standard response of "not bad". That's actually a pretty negative response, because it suggests that you expect things to be bad but today they are just slightly better than that. Next time someone asks you how you are, respond with, "I'm really good" or "I'm great, thanks". That will probably force them to ask why things are good or great and you can share something positive with them.

Valuing my own time

One of the biggest learnings along this journey has been to recognise the value of my own time. When I was trading my time for money in my job, I was paid a certain amount of money for prescribed hours. If I spent more hours doing that job, I would not necessarily get paid any more money, so my hourly rate would effectively go down. Then, when I bought my first couple of properties, I was so focused on keeping my expenditure as low as possible that I did most of the manual work myself, without ever considering the value of my own time. In reality, I could have earned more money if I had spent that time looking for more deals than by – again - trading my time for money at a much lower level than I could actually get doing something more worthwhile and more suited to my skills. Finding another great property deal to invest in could have earned me tens of thousands of pounds. Doing the labouring, decorating, etc. probably saved me a couple of thousand.

It's not always possible just to do the things that earn you the greatest amount of money, but having at least recognised the value of my time to do different things, I am now more selective and make a conscious effort to get the maximum return on my time. And you should always think in this way, yourself, as you go through your daily life. If you can earn £20 per hour for doing something you are good at and it costs £10 per hour to have someone cut the grass in your garden, then it makes sense to get a gardener, as long as you actually go out and do the thing that earns you the higher amount of money. Doing the gardening yourself will mean you avoid paying out £10, but you lose the time that you could have spent earning £20, i.e. it's a net loss of £10 an hour. It's a very simple concept but one that took a while to really sink in for me.

I really started to benefit from this understanding when I began earning very good rates to mentor other investors and could earn in a day what I might pay someone to manage my portfolio on a part-time basis for a month. Now, that really is leveraging my time and money to the maximum!

Just being paid higher sums of money gave me increased confidence because it was recognition of my skills and knowledge and a reflection of my value within the market. In the vast majority of jobs, the remuneration is a fairly standard market rate; there is a certain perceived value to the position you hold and so, unless you can increase the value you offer to the market, your pay will not increase. People who earn a lot of money usually create a lot of value within the job they perform. They bring something extra to the role that not many other people could, and this 'rarity factor' makes them more valuable. You, therefore, need to develop as an individual before you can rightly ask for more money. In the world of business, those businesses that create the most value for the marketplace earn a massive amount of money themselves.

Having developed so much as a person over the last 5 years, I sometimes wish I had known then what I know now. That's obviously not possible and we can only do what we do at any time with the knowledge that we have at that point. The most important thing is to put into practice all the things you learn along the way and continue to grow and develop. One of my favourite sayings from Brian Tracy is, "always be a moving target". In essence, it means that you should always keep taking action, keep developing as a person and keep building your business. There will be plenty of people that will want to shoot you down or overtake you, but as long as you keep moving you can stay ahead of the competition. I like to try new things and there are always fresh goals to be set and new targets to be achieved.

Most of my friends that knew me when I first started on my property investment journey say I have changed a lot – for the better! - and some of my old school friends that I have got back in touch with are impressed with what I have achieved as well. But I have also had a few of them say they wish that they had done what I did back then, but feel they have now missed the boat, and some say that I just got lucky. That's the nature of people – there will always be those who view other people's success with a degree of envy, bitterness or negativity and simply can't accept that they got there not by luck or 'happy circumstance', but by sheer determination and hard work. Fortunately, those people are in the minority and you quickly learn who to steer clear of.

Remember that you cannot change and become better at something unless you're prepared to take a risk. I recall feeling so far out of my comfort zone at the time I was doing my mentoring with Steve that, for a brief moment, I wanted to go back to how things were before, even though I had a real desire to do something different. Change is scary and taking on new challenges can be hard, but I am *so* glad now that I took that risk, got educated and put what I had learned into practice, because, believe me, I'm getting the rewards for doing so now.

Chapter 9

My life today

The last five years have been quite a journey for me and I see myself now in a completely different way to how I saw myself back then. Being an employee, with an employee mentality, and not really having a plan to work to or any goals, was not going to help me get to where I wanted. It's a common human condition to accept our circumstances, take the card we think life has dealt us and get on with things, but it's actually possible for everyone to make changes to their life and do something different.

A very inspirational speaker that I have had the great pleasure of listening to a couple of times is the blind adventurer, Miles Hilton-Barber. One of Miles' great sayings is, "It's not the blowing of the wind that determines your destination in life; it's the set of your sails". He encourages us to not let outside conditions affect the way we live our lives, because those are things we can't control. Instead, we should concentrate on what we *can* control, i.e. ourselves. You can set your sails differently and go down a different path - don't just be carried along with everyone else. Take control of your circumstances and change them, if you so wish.

I can remember when I was looking at buying my first investment property, I didn't really consider that I could get any further than that first purchase. It was such a major hurdle for me at the time and the looming learning curve seemed so steep, that I couldn't really see any further ahead than that. What I have learnt since is that sometimes you just need to focus on a big target, not worry too much about the specifics of how you're going to get there and not let challenges along the way block your vision for the longer term. Even though when you set that target you may have no idea of how you are going to achieve it, nothing should stop you from setting the target in the first place. It's amazing the number of times things just fall into place when you need them, as long as you have that belief and knowledge that you *will* reach your ultimate target and achieve the big goals. You can't plan for all eventualities and there are always going to be unexpected hiccups along the way, but you just need to get on with things and make sure you're in a position to make the right decisions when you need to.

The main reason I wanted to get involved in property investing in the first place was to change my own financial circumstances - money was probably the key motivator. But I also knew that property would be something I would enjoy, and that has played a massive part in my success, because I don't think I would have been prepared to make some of the sacrifices I have, or put in the long hours and hard work, if it didn't enjoy what I do. When you truly enjoy the business that you are in or the job that you do, it shouldn't feel like work. I can honestly say that for the majority of the last five years, the work that I've been doing hasn't felt like a job, but just become a normal part of what I do every day. That's maybe just a small difference in perception, but it's how I see things and that's made a massive difference in terms of how I've grown and developed as a person and as a business owner.

In the last couple of years, money has become less important - although I am aware that perhaps that's a luxury I can afford to feel, now that I have a decent income and standard of living! What I really mean is that money for money's sake is no longer a key motivator. Some people want money purely so they can buy things, accumulate possessions and go on expensive holidays – so they can look wealthier than other people. But being successful has given me two things which I value more highly than 'money': freedom and choice. And, ultimately, I think that's what most people would want to have in their life - money is just the thing that facilitates those luxuries.

What freedom and choice mean to me

Freedom is about having the financial freedom and time freedom to be able to control what I do and not be governed by other people. Financial freedom doesn't mean you have to be a millionaire. It simply means that you have enough money coming in on a fairly passive basis to be able to support yourself financially and don't have to directly trade your time for money in a job in order to keep paying the bills. There are many other property investors that have significantly more wealth and income than I do, but it's not a competition. It's about your own circumstances and what's right for you. Yes, we would all like more income and more wealth, but we all start from different points and, as long as you are improving your position, then that's what matters. In terms of time freedom, there is nothing better than having full control of your own diary, not having to do things or be in certain places at certain times, with someone else dictating your schedule, but being able to prioritise how you split your time between the things that matter most to you. Of course, I still have days when I need to be in a certain place at a certain time - that's just life and even the most successful people in the world have that - but I usually have the freedom to be able to fit external demands around my other appointments, interests and activities.

Choice is about really having the ability to make decisions freely. When you are able to make big decisions, you are more in control of your own life. Choosing to be able to spend more time with friends and family is fantastic. Having a choice about when you work - whether you take some time off during the day to go out for a run or choose to work through an evening so you can have a morning off - means you have the flexibility to do what you want, when you want and with whom you want. At work, most people end up spending a lot of time with people that they don't necessarily like. When you have the luxury of being able to choose, though, you can spend your time with people that you genuinely get along with. I don't now work with anyone that I don't truly like and trust.

Without money I don't believe you can have true freedom and choice – and those are the things I've grown to really value - so my focus now is absolutely on the *benefits* money can bring, rather than just making money for the sake of accumulating zeros in the bank.

It's that focus on the benefits that has helped me move forwards and continually seek to grow my business, knowing I'm doing it for the right reasons. Many of the great business leaders, such as Bill Gates, work tirelessly in their enterprises and continue to make billions of pounds each year. Some argue that they are just being greedy, when, in truth, they do it so that the money can benefit more and more people. Their business empires provide jobs and financial security for thousands of people; their personal income means their family will have lifelong freedom and choice, and they tend to also use their wealth for the greater good. Bill Gates set up his foundation so that he could help those less fortunate and share the benefits of his wealth. When he dies, the vast majority of his wealth and fortune will be given away to charity.

While we're not all in a position to be quite as generous as Bill Gates, it is important to share your wealth with friends, family and those less fortunate. I make donations to local charities, raised money for Barnardo's when I ran the London Marathon in 2010 and always try to support friends and family whenever they are raising money for charities that they want to help. It isn't a competition as to who can do the most, but it is important to recognise the positive impact you can have on other people and the difference you can make, if you are in a strong enough position. Being able to help others is a privilege and certainly something that motivates me to grow my business and increase profitability.

Completing the 2010 London marathon was one of my biggest personal achievements, but in the last few years I have also completed the 3 Peaks Challenge and jumped out of a plane at 12,000 ft. Some of the challenges were to raise money for charity and some were just personal challenges that I wanted to do. I have now applied to run the New York marathon this year and hopefully can combine a bit of a holiday with the completion of another personal challenge along the way. I like these fitness challenges because they keep me focused on another target to beat that is outside the business sphere, plus they keep me healthy.

I am always amazed when people seek to make a lot of money only to be completely unhealthy and overweight at the same time. I think that financial wealth and personal health should be very closely aligned. What's the point in having lots of money if you don't look after yourself and are potentially shortening the life you have? I work with a personal trainer once a week and enjoy having him there to push me to do more and get fitter. I have never been a fan of going to the gym and find it difficult to really motivate myself to take regular exercise, so having a personal trainer works well for me. We went out running together the other day at 2 o'clock in the afternoon on a weekday, with the sun shining, and it really made me appreciate having the freedom and choice to be able to exercise when and where I like, because I couldn't think of anything better to have being doing at that time.

I now also take more time off with my wife and we go on more holidays than we used to. Another major benefit of having a business that is structured so that it effectively runs without me on a day-to-day basis, means that I can be practically anywhere in the world and it still operates without me. My staff know that if there's a problem, they only need to phone, email or text – I'm always on the end of my BlackBerry! I sometimes need to take a few hours here and there to check in with deals and projects back home, but that's a small price to pay for the increased number of breaks my wife and I can take, and it really doesn't interfere with my enjoyment of my holiday. Last year I had my first skiing and sailing holidays and am now looking forward to doing more of those activities. The desktop background on my laptop is of a picture of the Balearic Islands that we sailed round last summer, and that reminds me every day of the fact that I want to go and do more of that. It's very similar to my vision board, but is on my laptop instead.

The structure and set-up of my business has changed a lot over the time that I have been growing it. Many small business owners find it difficult to remove themselves from the day-to-day running of the business and never really get to the point of time freedom, which was probably one of the reasons they wanted to start their own business in the first place. Being part of a franchise network but also learning from other more experienced business people and by reading about other successful investors I have recognised the huge benefit of systemising a business & learnt how to do that so that it can run without me on a day to day basis. I still spend a few hours each week working 'in' the business, but the vast majority of my time is now spent working either 'on' the business or doing other things, such as finding more property deals, finding other investors to work with and making contacts in the property sector, etc. I choose to work from home more often than not, which means my team get used to me not being around and know that they can get on with their jobs without me looking over their shoulder every five minutes. It also demonstrates that I trust my team to get on with their jobs and gives them the responsibility to develop their role and the daily running of the business so that we all benefit from it.

My fellow franchise partners and the other contacts and affiliates that I surround myself with tend to have real strengths and skills, gained from their former careers, in areas of business where I am weaker. By networking and doing business with these people, my own property business has been helped immensely, as I have benefitted from their expertise in financial management, recruitment, lettings management, people management, etc. My plan is not to grow a huge organisation but to keep the business small, lean and efficient enough to be able to run my property portfolio successfully. Ultimately, my property portfolio is still my responsibility, but I know I have good people working with me that can operate the business and make a success of it.

It is now about four years since I left full time employment. I'll never forget that 'Sunday night' feeling where you know the weekend is over and it's back to work in the morning. I'm sure you've all felt that at some point...and perhaps you still feel it today. I am so grateful that feeling has now gone for me and I know it's gone for good. More often than not, my weekdays and weekends just blend into one – a week is simply a week and all 7 days are there to be used for whatever I want and need them for, which means that I look forward to the days ahead. I hear people talk about 'a work-life balance', but work and life just become one when you love what you do. Why separate work from 'life'? Make work or business part of what you do every day and then it doesn't become something that you dread. As Donald Trump has said, "If you're interested in 'balancing' work and pleasure, stop trying to balance them. Instead make your work more pleasurable."

I have some days where my diary is packed out with things and then days where it's empty. I don't get stressed about having days where I am less busy because, as I've already said, I would rather be productive when I need to be, rather than just busy for the sake of it. Having days that are less hectic is great because it actually allows you time to think and plan what you are going to do next. Busy, packed diaries normally mean that you end up going from one thing to the next, because it says you have to, without ever allowing yourself the space to really think. I know some business people that thrive on being really busy for periods of time and then completely shut off and go on holiday for a few months each year. Personally, I prefer to take shorter, more regular breaks. The important thing is to know what works best for you and then put that into practice, but do make sure you give yourself time to recharge and space to think and plan. I am certainly more productive when I plan what I am going to do and then, if I get it done more quickly than I thought (which happens quite often), I take more time to plan the next thing for me to do, rather than race to fill my day with another task.

My comfort zone is now so much bigger than it was five years ago and it really is a comfortable place to be. But that's not the end. Once you begin to realise how much you can develop as a person, it becomes a never-ending journey, as you begin to really enjoy doing the things that stretch you. I now love the thought of tackling new challenges, because I know they'll benefit me in lots of different ways and I'm excited about seeing the results. In terms of property, I'd now like to learn how to invest in a professional way in commercial property and understand the mechanics of property development. Property is something that I know and that I enjoy doing, and it's easy to keep up the enthusiasm and appetite for it because there are so many different angles and strategies that you can look at, once you've got your core business set up. As with my HMO investing journey, I am beginning to network with possible mentors and other people who have been successful in the commercial and development sectors that I can learn from and short cut my route to success in those areas.

I am now surrounded by successful people who are all developing and growing their businesses. Being around like-minded people is key to having a support network that you can rely on when things get tough. Every day is not sweetness and light, so to be able to pick up the phone and speak to someone who understands, and has probably been through the same challenges and come out the other side, really does help. I meet on a regular basis with other franchise partners from around the country, and hearing and seeing other people be successful also helps to inspire me to do more. And it's great to be able to share my stories and experiences with those that are behind me on the same journey and help them develop in certain areas, as I benefitted from people helping me when I was at that stage. Even if it's just one piece of information or advice they need, it's a very rewarding thing to be able to share that with them and help them move forwards.

While I've been writing this book there have been many stories on the news about the negative state of the economy: speculation about when interest rates might go up to stop inflation getting out of control; news that retirement ages have been increased so people will have to work for longer; reports that pension pots are not going to deliver the income that people need to survive in later life; statistics showing unemployment figures are rising; warnings that energy prices will continue to rise, etc. All doom and gloom, as per normal! While some of that will undoubtedly affect me, it is great to know that actually I am more in control of my future than any other person or outside influence. I now feel confident that I have a very robust business model and the skills and the knowledge to be able to survive and thrive through whatever economic conditions are likely to lie ahead of us.

Setting down the details of my journey so far has been truly enjoyable and helped remind me of the key moments that have made a real difference to me – business-wise and personally.

I wonder at times where I would be now and what I would be doing if I had not made the decision to change the path that I was heading along five years ago. Some people ask me where I think I'll be in another five years from now, and I really do struggle to come up with an answer. I would never have predicted that I could achieve everything I have already, so I feel like my future is even more uncertain. For now, I am happy taking things year by year and planning ahead on a 12 month basis, and I have absolutely no doubt that my next book covering years five to ten will be even more satisfying to write than this one!

We usually overestimate our short-term goals and underestimate our long-term goals, so while you can't expect to be a millionaire overnight, it's amazing what you can achieve in the long term with persistence and gentle progress. I'm living proof that if you make small, consistent steps in the right direction, over a period of time you will make a massive difference to your life.

"It's not the blowing of the wind that determines your destination in life; it's the set of your sails."
Miles Hilton-Barber

PART TWO

2014: Looking back & moving forward

Chapter 10
Reflections

It's nearly three years since I started writing this book and about two and a half years since it was first published. I initially thought I'd leave it at least five years before writing any more, but both I and my investment strategy have undergone some significant changes recently, so I wanted to update this book and share with you what I've been up to.

I also wanted to take the opportunity to thank those of you that bought the first edition (2011) and are now reading this new section. I've received some amazing emails and social media messages from readers who have been inspired by my story and gone out and taken positive action as a result; for me, it's a fantastic feeling to know I've helped someone with their own journey. That's why I enjoy mentoring new investors and one of the key objectives I had for writing the book. Many of the reviews left on sites like Amazon have been great to read – you may even have read them yourself and bought the book as a direct result! It's been incredible to see how shared feedback across different platforms has enabled me to reach a much wider audience than I had ever hoped.

At the same time, I'd like to respond to some of the negative comments and reviews. They say 'you can't please all of the people all of the time' and that certainly seems to have been the case with my book! I always welcome constructive criticism, but there were some comments that really made me laugh. Of the less ridiculous complaints, most seemed to have stemmed from readers' unrealistic expectations of what they would learn.

This book was never intended to be a 'how to' guide. It doesn't say anywhere that it is; it's simply the story of how I was able to leave my job and get into property investing full time: by following a system and putting in the required time and effort. It would be almost impossible to do a step-by-step blueprint for my investment journey and – even if I could - I don't believe it would be very helpful. The level of detail needed to describe exactly how I did everything would make it one of the thickest property investment books out there and that's simply not the most effective way to get that sort of information across. Property investment is a people business and an ever-shifting market, in which no two situations are exactly the same. So, while books can undoubtedly give you some very useful information and an excellent insight into what's needed to run a successful property business, they can't teach you all the skills.

If you are interested in specific details and would like to get some one-to-one help, then please get in touch. If I can't help you directly myself, I should be able to point you in the right direction.

Personal changes

For the last 18 months or so, I have not been as active in my property business as I was in the first five or six years but, for me, that's what it's all about and the reason I worked so hard in those early days. I am keen to continue developing myself and my business, but very much through working smartly and doing the best rather than the most deals.

My journey through property has been an amazing and life-changing experience – not only for me, but also for my immediate family. We are in a much more comfortable position now than I am sure we would have been if I hadn't got started in property when I did and received the kind of help I've had along the way. I talked at the end of the first edition (Part One) of the book about the two main things that property investing had given me - freedom and choice - and those became more important than ever before in 2012, when I became a father for the first time.

For those of you reading this book who have kids of your own, I don't need to tell you how much they change your life. We are all doing well, growing up together, and I've been able to spend a lot of time with my son in these important early days, months and years. This, more than anything, has brought home to me the value of having a business that doesn't need me to be there all the time. Many of my friends regret not being able to spend more time with their young kids but they, as many people do, have jobs for which they need to be out from early in the morning until late at night. Thanks to how I've systemised my property business, I'm able to regularly take my son to nursery in the mornings and am proud to have played an active part in the early part of his life. I'm not trying to show off, I'm just highlighting how ultimately worthwhile all those personal sacrifices I had to make while I focused on growing the business were. The investment I made, working long hours every day, giving up 'free time' and foregoing material things, is now paying me back many times over, in the form of being able to spend plenty of quality time with my family, doing things that we enjoy.

In the last 18 months or so, I have also often found myself with time on my hands and recognised that it's a nice place to be. At times I have thought I should be pushing myself harder and filling my day with more projects, more activities, more deals, more challenges, etc. but I've chosen not to. Instead, I focus on being as productive as possible in the areas that give the most value to me & my business; I continue to work hard, but I place just as much importance on life outside work. Just one of the things I'm really pleased about is that I've been able to play more golf than ever before - sometimes three times a week - and have brought down my handicap quite significantly…at last!

But it's not just me that's moved on…

Changes in the property market

As I write this, we are in a very interesting period for economic recovery in general and the property market in particular. Every report, index or future forecast says the property market is on the way up. For some areas this is yet to really kick in, but for others it has been happening for a while. The Government's Help to Buy scheme may be fuelling some of that, but it's important to remember that it is also the nature of markets to go up and down over time and the property market has peaked and troughed relatively regularly since records began – it is cyclical. The basic principles of supply and demand mean that when those two things are out of sync, as they are now, prices move, and a strong demand for people to own their own home, together with a shortage of properties being built or sold on the open market, will always lead to price rises.

If the market really picks up momentum then I'm sure the Bank of England will put up interest rates to try to slow price rises, but it will be difficult to judge the strength of the economy on that basis, as many people have simply got far too used to such a low base rate. They may also pull back on some of the other funding programmes they have put in place in recent years to try and support banks, make lending easier and kick start the much-needed scale of new development that is needed to match the continued demand for housing in this country. It's funny how quickly people forget about the past - when the market peaked in 2007 & 2008, many were saying that we would never again see prices and mortgage LTVs at such high levels. Well, we undoubtedly will and, in some cases, both are already there!

If you are looking to invest in a rising market, it's important to act quickly but do be aware that there are still good deals to be done; don't get caught in the hype and overpay for properties. If the market continues to rise, it will save you, but if it tails off and goes down again, that is not a nice position to be in.

If you are an existing investor, the likelihood of interest rate rises means you will need to keep an eye on them. If you have any tracker mortgages, you'll currently be getting a great deal, but have you worked out your break-even point should (or when) rates rise? Are you comfortable with that figure? Are there opportunities for you to look at taking a fixed-rate mortgage now that will insulate you against future rises? Speak to a mortgage broker and get their advice and thoughts on what options may be available to you.

I will certainly be looking closely at mortgages in 2014 and working out some numbers based on my current portfolio and rent versus interest payments. Rates will only go up in the immediate future but you will usually pay a premium for the privilege of securing the best rates, so it's important you factor in all the costs you would incur in changing mortgage products and calculate whether that would be the right move for you.

Reflecting on my strategy

When I look back at my HMO property investment journey, there are two things that stand out for me as real achievements: mastering a business strategy and reaching a level of financial freedom. It was the challenge of securing those two things that drove me and excited me.

The best bit about having a system where you can 'turn the key' and quickly and easily convert one property into something that more-or-less matches another asset you already own and conforms to a proven business model is that it makes the job simple and less challenging. But that's also the worst bit. Being focused and targeted is great, but when something stops being a challenge, you can quickly become bored and lose interest. That's what happened to me after five or six years and I realised I needed to set myself new, different targets that would provide new challenges and reignite my passion for making property deals.

And so, over the last 18 months, I have moved away from HMOs and into the commercial market, which has been quite an experience: exciting, frustrating, challenging and profitable – all in equal measure! The model for investing in HMOs still works brilliantly when done correctly – and I continue to recommend it as a great foundation for a portfolio and the single best strategy for realising good, on-going income - but now I have much greater interest in finding other, new ways to profit from property. Unless something amazing comes to the market or there are a number of properties being sold together by another landlord, then I think my days of acquiring individual HMOs are behind me.

That being said, I continue to make use of my HMO skills and knowledge in assessing the options for developing commercial premises, and I'm grateful to have that in my 'repertoire', as it enables me to see potential in a property that those who have a more 'conventional' approach might miss. Converting offices into multiple occupancy residential accommodation is a strategy that offers the potential for superb returns.

What I've learned from all this is the importance of reassessing your strategy and not allowing your business to become stale. When you lose interest, that's when things start to slip, so you must make sure you don't fall into the trap of becoming too comfortable. Revisit your strategy occasionally to make sure it's still helping you meet your goals – both financial and personal - and that it really is giving you the rewards you're looking for.

Chapter 11

Change is a constant

There's always something happening when you own a property portfolio. Whether it's issues with tenants or issues with the properties themselves, very rarely does everything go smoothly and tick along for any length of time without challenges being thrown at you. And in the last couple of years I have had some new experiences that I think are worth sharing.

Extending short leases

As a general rule, you'll find it difficult to get a mortgage on anything with less than 60 years left on the lease and a solicitor is likely to flag up anything under 80 years. Consequently, in order to keep the values of any leasehold properties you own as high as possible, you must ensure that they have leases of a decent length.

A maisonette I own had a lease with just 68 years remaining. Using some of my contacts, I found a local surveyor that specialised in leasehold extension valuations and found out from him exactly how the process works. As long as you have owned the property for more than two years, you have the right to extend your lease, although, as the tenant, you also have to pay the legal costs of the freeholder, so it can be quite an expensive process. In addition, the shorter the lease gets, the more expensive it is likely to be to extend it. Nevertheless, I take the view that when you look at the cost as a percentage of the property value, it's well worth the outlay to ensure your asset is protected.

When I approached the freeholder, he thought he had the right to refuse me the extension. His intention had been to take back all the maisonettes in the block when their leases expired, so he could pass them on to his family, and I think it came as quite a shock to him to find out that his tenants had this right to extend. As a result, he tried to make the premium that I had to pay to extend the lease and all the additional costs as high as possible.

There is a tribunal process you can use if either party is being unreasonable but, in the end, we managed to avoid that and agreed a price to extend the lease for another 99 years, on top of the original remaining 68 years. That has now increased the value of the flat and made it much more saleable – if I ever want to sell. I have another leasehold maisonette that I'll be extending the lease on in 2014, and I'm hoping that the knowledge I gained through this first experience will make it a much easier process!

There is a lot of information on the internet about your right to extend your lease and, fortunately, the method for calculating the likely cost seems to be a set formula, using only a few variables, which makes the process relatively easy to understand. As with much in the property business, negotiating the extension will usually come down to a series of offers and counter-offers between you and the freeholder - you giving a low starting figure and them a high one - ending up with you agreeing to meet somewhere in the middle. Your landlord/freeholder may be a large property investment company used to dealing with these sorts of things, meaning you should be able to complete the process fairly quickly; or, as in my case, you may be dealing with an individual with no previous experience of extending a lease, which can make things quite difficult and result in a more lengthy negotiation. Either way, stick with it and remember that you're doing this to protect the value of your asset.

Dealing with problem tenants

Some tenants are more 'needy' than others and some cause more problems than others but, in general, I think we have done very well with the tenants we've selected for our properties. We haven't always got it right and it's important to be realistic about the fact that - particularly when you're dealing with large numbers of individual tenants, as you are with an HMO portfolio – some will slip under the radar, but with the systems and checks we have in place, we almost always manage to filter out the tenants that we feel are not right for us.

In house sharing situations it's especially important to try to select tenants who will not only pay you rent every month but also fit in with the other people in the house. That's hard, because you can only tell so much about a person when you show them the property and, although my lettings team and I seem to have pretty good gut instincts, we have occasionally had tenants who have turned out to be quite different from our initial impression. And no matter how well you screen tenants, there will always be the odd personality clash and argument. One of the good things about having multiple properties is that, if those kinds of situations escalate, you can usually offer to move someone to a different house.

But on one of the occasions when we got it wrong, it ended up costing me a lot of time and money. Most landlords' worst nightmare is having a tenant who stops paying their rent, refuses to leave and the matter ends up going to court – and that's exactly what happened to me.

The tenant rejected our offer to write off his debt to us if he simply left the property - even though he owed a lot of money – and refused to accept our reasoning that this would be the best solution for all of us. Instead, he chose to force us down the route of having to evict him via the courts, knowing that it would probably take a few months, which would buy him some time, even though it also meant he would incur more costs and increase his debt.

Fortunately, the court found in my favour and a date was set for him to leave the property. He chose to ignore this date, so we had to apply to the court again for bailiffs to call at the property to evict him. Just before this was due to happen, he vacated his room and gave up the keys to the property. He now has a County Court Judgement (CCJ) against him for the debt I am owed, which will stay on his record and come up in any credit check for up to six years. I can choose to proceed with that and seek for the money to be repaid or simply write it off as a bad debt and move on – at the moment I am still undecided which way to go. If someone genuinely doesn't have the money, it's pointless pursuing them; however, if they do and are simply choosing to avoid repaying the debt, that's different and I think it's probably worth taking action to recover your money.

In order to be properly prepared for a situation like this, you MUST have all your paperwork correct and up to date. I would also recommend you take professional advice and pay someone to ensure you always act 100% legally, because any error you make in your paperwork or in administering the eviction process can result in your case being delayed or even thrown out. And don't underestimate what a nerve-wracking experience it is going to court, especially if, as in my case, you haven't done anything like that before, so make sure you work with people that can guide and advise you.

Some landlords I've met have been able to reel off loads of bad tenant stories, but I'm glad to say I don't have very many. (I do have lots of hilarious stories, which could make for a very funny and quite lengthy book at some point!) I find that the vast majority of tenants are decent people and, in most cases, will contact you to let you know if they're going to have trouble paying their rent, either because they've lost their job or their circumstances have changed. As a landlord, it's important to appreciate tenants being honest and up front and to work closely with them from the moment problems arise to find the best solution for everyone. Remember, without tenants & the income they bring, most investments just don't work.

Maintaining and updating your properties

When you start out in property, assuming you're planning diligently, you'll budget for maintenance - some areas of the property, such as paintwork and appliances, will need regular maintenance, while others, such as furniture and the fabric of the building, will be periodical, longer-term considerations. I'm no longer surprised by the crazy things some tenants manage to do to properties and what items get broken in shared houses. However realistic you think you have been with your maintenance budget, there are always things that catch you out, so build in some sort of contingency.

HMOs suffer a much higher level of wear and tear than single-unit rentals and the longer you own them, the more maintenance they need. Carpets get worn out and dirty; walls get scraped when people are moving stuff in and out of rooms; kitchen worktops get marked or chipped with so many people using them, etc. This isn't damage you can attribute to any one individual; it is simply wear and tear from usage of the property by multiple people over a lengthy period of time. And if you want to keep attracting decent tenants who will pay a good level of rent, you have to stay on top of this kind of thing and budget accordingly for the cost of fixing or replacing these items.

In the last 18 months, all my properties have undergone a programme of maintenance and refurbishment on the communal areas, to make sure they look smart and modern. There are always newer properties coming onto the market, competing for tenants, so keep an eye on how other landlords are presenting their properties and make sure yours don't fall behind the market standard. And most tenants will appreciate you re-investing money back into a property, particularly those that have been there a while, because it's their home. Make sure it's a nice place for them to live and show them it matters to you that they are happy living there.

About nine months ago I got more involved in the day-to-day running of my business, to take a closer look at what was happening in some of the properties, and was surprised at what I found. I hadn't been inside many of them myself for a couple of years and had simply relied on the information in my team's weekly reports. What I discovered was that spreadsheets and reports will only give you a limited picture of what is really happening 'on the ground'.

I was surprised to see how poorly one particular property was being kept and that it wasn't because the tenants were treating it badly, but because we were not managing it correctly or maintaining it as well as we should have been. My weekly reports showed that we had been achieving pretty much full occupancy, with 100% rent collection each month, so, on paper, all had appeared to be fine.

I bumped into one of the tenants (who didn't know who I was) and told him I was inspecting the property for maintenance purposes. He said that because he lived in a shared house he didn't actually expect much of the property or think there was any reason why it should be well maintained. I was really shocked and disappointed that he felt renting a room meant he couldn't expect a decent standard of accommodation. I immediately went back to the office to find out from my team what was going on and why that property hadn't been maintained to our usual standards. It appeared that it had simply 'slipped through the net' because laziness had crept in and not all the processes had been stuck to.

Within a couple of weeks, the property was refurbished internally, with walls being plastered & decorated in the communal areas and a new bathroom suite, tiles and flooring. I went back after the work was completed and bumped into the same tenant, who was over the moon with the work we had done. I told him his comments had been taken to heart and thanked him for giving honest feedback without knowing what the after effects would be. Not only did the completed work make the existing tenants happier, but it also makes it easier to rent the property whenever a room becomes available – a win/win for everyone concerned.

The last couple of years have taught me that no matter how well you plan and systemise your property business, you can never walk away completely from the day-to-day operations. Great managers understand the grass roots of their business and appreciate that even the very best systems and strategies need re-evaluating from time to time. Change is both unavoidable and necessary in order to stay on top, so be prepared for it.

Chapter 12

A strategy shift

As I mentioned in Chapter 10, 2011 saw me make the decision to get into commercial property and development, which is a very different strategy from HMOs. When done correctly, multi-lets generate a profit every month and you get a payback on your investment straight away – it's very much a cash flow strategy. In contrast, commercial/development deals are capital projects, where you hope to make a much larger profit in one go on completion of that project, whether it be from selling a site with planning permission or developing a scheme and then selling the individual units. But from the moment you invest your capital, you may not get any return until you succeed in disposing of the asset – which can take many months or even years. That's why you need to ensure you have another form of income to finance your monthly outgoings in the meantime.

Funding these projects in the short term can be challenging when you factor in all the costs, but the rewards at the end should certainly make it worthwhile. On top of the purchase price of the site/unit, your initial capital plan needs to include: interest on the money you borrow, insurance, security (particularly if the building is empty), business rates, planning application fees, planning consultant & architect fees, legal fees & utility bills. In addition to all those material costs, I suggest you also factor in a value for your time and the anticipated length of the project and build in a reasonable contingency.

Although it's a big part of investing, raising the necessary capital has actually been the least of my problems. It's the process that has frustrated me, with a number of failed deals along the way, and I'd like to share some of my learnings with you.

Attempt #1: 'the perfect deal'!

In May 2011, I found what looked like the perfect opportunity for a profitable commercial venture in Chelmsford. The premises were two office buildings that had been internally merged into one. The buildings were empty and the owner was selling at a reasonable price, plus the location was great, close to the train and bus stations and the city centre. Everything looked promising.

I approached another investor with the proposition that if they bought one unit, I could buy the other and then my company could manage the whole process, from refurbishment to tenanting and managing the properties. We agreed a price and went 'sale agreed', subject to us getting planning permission for change of use from offices to residential. The owner was happy with this and agreed to take the property off the market while we went through the planning application process. It was highly likely we would get planning, as the offices had originally been houses anyway, so we were effectively only reverting to the original use class, rather than applying for something completely different.

We received planning permission from the local authority within the expected timescale and were all set to exchange and complete shortly after. And then the vendor and his solicitor went quiet on us.

If you aren't aware, planning permission sits with the property and not with the applicant. Regardless of who submits the application, once approved it then sits with the current owner of the property - and at that time that wasn't me! Our major error was accepting the vendor's word, rather than fixing it into the contract that he would wait for us to get planning permission and then sell to us. Looking back, I knew we were taking a risk to do it that way but I suppose, not having done this sort of deal before, it wasn't something I gave a huge amount of thought to.

It very quickly became apparent that there was another buyer waiting in the wings; the vendor withdrew our contract and sold the property to this other buyer for £40,000 more than we had agreed to pay. At the time, I was gutted that I had not only missed out on what would have been a great deal, but also wasted my time and money submitting the planning application and completing the legal process up to the point of exchange. Factoring in the 'lost' income that I'd planned to achieve, it became an even bigger mistake, but the only thing I could do was put it down to experience and learn from it.

Since then, I've realised that because there is real value in changing the use of a site and maximising its potential, good deals are hard to find, as many people now factor the 'potential' into their asking price. While I completely understand sellers not wanting to undervalue their asset, this 'inflated valuation' really doesn't take into account the risk and costs incurred by the buyer in going through a planning application process with an uncertain outcome.

Attempt #2: Failed negotiations

With the lessons learned from my first attempt at a commercial deal very much at the forefront my mind, when I found another potentially suitable deal, one of the first things I discussed with the vendor - even before talking about the price - was making the deal subject to obtaining planning permission. But they weren't happy to have that form part of the contract, nor were they willing to budge from the asking price, so I had to think a bit more creatively.

These were office premises, close to the city centre and on a busy junction, but with a great layout that could reasonably easily be converted into mainly residential accommodation with some office space. It would have been ideal for us to use ourselves as a new base for the business, so I was keen to find a way to make it work.

I proposed a kind of 'lease option' agreement, where I would rent the building from the current owners while I got my planning permission in place, with an option to purchase the property at the end of the agreed rental period. We started putting together a Heads of Terms agreement, outlining how the deal would work, only for the vendors to then change their mind and say they wanted a straight purchase deal or nothing. Again, looking back, I can't help wondering whether I should have just bought the property anyway and taken a risk on whether my planning application would be successful. But you can only do what you feel is right at the time and, having been burned by my first experience, I wanted to be a bit more cautious. This was at the end of 2011 / start of 2012 and the property has only recently (end of 2013) gone under offer, so I think walking away was probably the right move. You will always be disappointed when a deal doesn't work out, but rest assured that if you look hard enough and make enough enquiries, there will be another deal out there that's right for you.

(In May 2013, the Government relaxed the planning laws for this kind of development and made it easier to apply under 'permitted development', rather than requiring a full planning application. Some London boroughs are challenging this decision in the High Court, but, in the meantime, there are many people applying to convert office space into residential accommodation under these new, relaxed laws. It is certainly more complex than the HMO strategy and funding is harder to get, but the returns can be phenomenal.)

I was now getting quite frustrated and realised that if I was going to succeed with this new strategy, I would have to take some more time to work out the best way to approach it. As I was fixed on only one investment location, I knew the number of opportunities coming up for sale at the right price would be very limited, particularly if I was only considering office buildings. So I decided I needed to explore more avenues.

The well-known property sites, such as Rightmove, will give you a small amount of information on available commercial properties, but you also need to contact commercial agents directly, as many only advertise on their own websites or other commercially-focused sites.

It was from one of these specialist commercial property sites that I found my next opportunity - a pub! Not quite what I was initially looking for, but by then I was prepared to widen my search criteria and be open to all possibilities. Although I didn't know anything about investing in pubs, it was actually only a couple of minutes' walk from where I live, so at least I had the comfort of knowing the area, and the price looked good. It had already ceased trading as a pub (as many have these days, due changes in drinking habits and the smoking ban) and, after viewing it, I started to think about what might be possible to achieve with it.

My initial thoughts were that it could be converted into flats or perhaps even a couple of houses – the big risk, again, would be whether I could get planning permission. Unfortunately, before I could get very far in my thoughts, it was sold to someone who simply moved on it more quickly than me. While widening your search criteria opens up new and different opportunities, it also presents you with more variables and more questions, and I simply couldn't answer them or work out a plan quickly enough. I realised that I needed to expand my range of contacts to include people who could help me with these sorts of properties.

Attempt #3: Success at last! (and more challenges along the way...)

By September 2012, I had spent more than twelve months trying to secure my first commercial property deal, with no success, when another pub in my local area came up for sale. It was being marketed at a good price and had a decent-sized plot, so I knew there was an opportunity there – I just didn't know exactly what it was!

I went and viewed the property and came away excited but also nervous about how to move forward. About a year earlier I had met a contact via LinkedIn, who was also into property, specifically commercial projects, such as hotels, B&Bs, wedding venues and care homes. We had agreed that, should a potential joint project come up, we would be in touch, so I picked up the phone and told him about the pub.

He came out to see the property with me and within three minutes said it looked like a good deal and that we should buy it! Much as with my previous experiences of learning from someone that had been there and done HMO investing before, he gave me the confidence to go ahead with the deal and jointly take on the risk of getting planning permission afterwards. I was really stretching my comfort zone, not only by buying a different type of property, but also by working closely with a new partner on a very different kind of project.

You could call it good or bad timing, but I was going on holiday with my family the next day, so had to leave it up to my business partner to secure the deal for us. He managed to negotiate a good reduction on the asking price and we were 'sale agreed' by the time I came home.

We made very slow progress in the actual buying of the property and came across an obstacle that nearly made the whole deal fall down. The issue related to an easement on the property and ownership and rights of way on surrounding bits of land. Luckily, our solicitor discovered it before we exchanged contracts, but it meant we had to come up with a solution to the problem fairly quickly, as it was starting to put pressure on the deal.

We had already spent some time putting together a plan of what we could do with the site, our preferred option being getting permission to demolish everything currently on the site and replace it all with housing. In one of my previous jobs, working for the local council, I had come into contact with a number of the planning officers and - again thanks to LinkedIn - I was able to reconnect with someone based in Chelmsford who I knew could help us and who I knew I would also enjoy working with. This planning consultant gave us his opinion of the site, its potential and an idea of the market for resale, then, with this in mind, we chose an architect that we knew did a lot of work for a client who would be one of our main targets for selling the site. With our planning consultant and architect in place, we started coming up with different options and configurations for the site, including keeping the existing building and extending and converting it to provide flats or even one or two HMOs.

After some negotiations, we overcame the problem of land ownership and the easement by agreeing to sell the site to the adjoining landowner once we had secured planning permission to develop it. We exchanged and completed on the deal in March 2013 and began to put together our final thoughts on what planning application we were going to make. The next step would then be to see what the Council thought and try to find a solution that worked for all parties.

Six months later - and after many meetings, phone calls and emails - we finally received permission to demolish the pub and replace it with six flats and four houses. This meant we could now sell the property and walk away with a good profit, not having got our hands dirty at all. It was a strange experience, as I had never sold a property before, but it was great to complete a commercial development project and (although we did overspend, and that's something I now know to keep an eye on in future) make a decent lump sum out of it. Not only that, but I have come away having gained more property experience, a good architect and planning consultant that I know I can rely on for further projects, and a trusted investment partner for the future.

I would love to do a couple of these deals every year and will continue to focus on this strategy throughout 2014, with the intention of one day keeping and developing a site for myself. But that's still a little while off – I do like to take things one step at a time!

Chapter 13

Looking to the future

I really enjoyed project managing the pub deal, as it gave me some new challenges and also helped me learn about elements of property of which I had no prior experience. Topographical surveys, judicial review periods for planning permissions, easements, etc. are all part of the process of gaining planning for sites and they're things that I now know to look out for in the future. I found it amazing at times how slowly things moved, although I am told that our project actually ran quite quickly because I was constantly pushing it along. Six months to buy a site and get planning permission approved is doing well, apparently!

The nature of the process with commercial/development-type deals means they're not all-consuming projects that require daily attention. While there is still a lot of work to do, different projects will progress at different speeds so, assuming you have a trusted team in place to help you, there is scope to run a number of them alongside each other – and that's something I'm looking forward to doing.

One of my key projects for 2014 is to purchase office premises for my business that offers extra space for residential conversion or for multi-occupancy business use. To me, there appears to be a gap in the market for the provision of small offices for businesses that are too big to be run from home, but not yet profitable enough to be able to afford serviced office space. I enjoy looking at how I can adapt the HMO model to create new opportunities and this is something I am in the early stages of researching within my local area.

Property certainly gives me what I want in terms of income and return on capital, but I also really enjoy exploring the versatility of it as an investment vehicle. It excites me to learn about different ways of making money from property and I love that you can go from 'just okay' to 'great' rewards by coming at an opportunity from a different angle.

Good financial planning

All the current talk about property prices rising really highlights to me the power of the degree of leverage you have with property that simply doesn't exist in most other industries. The fact that you can borrow up to 95% of a property's value and only have to contribute 5% yourself is nothing new, but when you then hear that prices might rise by 5% per annum and you factor in that growth - not just on your 5%, but on the whole asset value – you've doubled your money in a year and that's an absolutely phenomenal return!

And that's the great thing about borrowing from a bank: when the market rises, their equity stays at the same level, while yours increases. When you then start to multiply these figures as you grow your portfolio, it gets really impressive. On a £2m portfolio, 5% growth per annum will add £100,000 to your asset value each year – and you haven't had to do anything. If that portfolio is mortgaged, the return on your actual cash invested will be something crazy, even factoring in the interest charged by the lender.

Of course, the reverse happens in a falling market, as many investors have experienced in recent years, and that is not a nice thing to watch, particularly as you have no control over what the 'market' does. Gaining or losing asset value on paper does not instantly give you any more or less cash in your pocket, but it does affect your loan to value (LTV) and how much equity you have. In a falling market, you may find yourself 'trapped' in a high LTV mortgage deal, but when the market rises again – as it almost always does – the increase in your asset value may enable you to refinance and access the extra equity. You can then either take it as a lump sum yourself, or reinvest it in growing your portfolio, which is what I have done.

This week I watched a television documentary about the 'pensions time bomb' we're facing, as people are living longer and either not paying enough into their pension plans or simply leaving it too late to start saving in the first place. Essentially, the programme was highlighting the fact that most people won't have enough money to live on in their retirement.

Pensions are a complicated area, full of jargon and small print, and when people don't fully understand something, they tend to simply shy away from it. Property, on the other hand, appears to be much easier to understand for most people.

Many already invest in property because they understand that house prices generally rise over time and they enjoy being able to watch their net worth increase as the years go by. Whether the plan is to release equity or cash in their asset down the line, or to take monthly income from letting, it seems that many people prefer to invest in something they understand and have more control over, rather than simply trusting their future financial security to a pension fund manager.

Making sure you and your family are covered for later life is one of your responsibilities. Leaving it to chance and relying on the Government is just not an option any more; the state pension – if there is still such a thing by the time many of us retire – is certainly not going to give you anything like the lifestyle you might be anticipating. It is hard to put money away today, especially when the cost of living is going up almost daily, but we have to accept that we need to take charge of our own financial future.

It will soon be my 35th birthday, which seems a very long way from retirement, and it still seems odd talking about pensions. To be quite honest with you, thoughts about my specific pension provision are still very much at the back of my mind. I invest for today and for the income that property provides, but I also know that my property assets will keep my family financially secure for the long term and provide my wife and I with a suitable 'pension plan'. I haven't yet addressed the issue of inheritance planning for my son, but I am aware I will need to start thinking about that soon. If you are a slightly older investor, bear in mind you will need to take specialist advice and put the right plans and documentation in place to ensure that those who may inherit your assets are properly looked after.

It is funny, looking at the last few paragraphs of the original book, that I spoke at the time about news of possible interest rate rises, pension problems, utility bills going up, etc....Sound familiar?! I think the main difference between now and two and a half years ago is the general confidence that the economy is starting to recover. Rather than interest rate rises to stop inflation, we are now talking about interest rates rising to stop the economy growing too fast. If the outlook remains positive and there is a confidence in the market, that can only be a good thing as it encourages further investment.

In my local area, I am seeing more and more developments happening and buildings coming out of the ground, which is fantastic. There are always the usual concerns about the impact on local infrastructure, but I would rather have the investment than not. We are certainly not back to the heady days of 2007, when the economy and the property market were booming, but at least we appear to be going in the right direction.

Property aside...

Moving forward...while I'm going to maintain my HMO portfolio and continue to seek out commercial projects, I am also open to looking at other business ventures. Although I have no idea yet what those may be, I have no doubt that the right project will present itself to me at the right time – hopefully something that will allow me to use my property and business development experience to make a success of a something in a completely different industry. Having a variety of business interests and different income streams helps keep things fresh, and I recognise that it's also sensible to spread risk through diversifying my asset portfolio.

I still enjoy keeping fit and have now been going to the same gym for six years. I'm currently training four times a week in a small group, rather than one to one, and am really enjoying the variety of doing spinning, boxing and high-intensity circuit training with different people each week. I follow certain trainers on Twitter that set their followers regular challenges, so that I have different targets to hit each month.

If you aren't active on the usual social media channels – Twitter, LinkedIn, Facebook, etc. – you're missing out! There are so many opportunities and contacts you can make through the virtual world that can help you in all aspects of your life, so I would really recommend that you take advantage of what this form of communication can offer you.

Finally, thank you for reading all this. I sincerely hope it's been helpful to learn about my journey and that you are now somewhere on the path to financial freedom yourself. Enjoy life and make sure you're always looking forward: to new and exciting challenges and the many happy times that lie ahead.

Ten Tips for Success

Set short and long term goals. Do this for you, personally, and also for your business if you have one. With some specific targets and goals you can really take control of the direction you are going in.

Write lists. Be organised and write down the things you need to do each day. It helps you stay on track and when you can see a record at the end of the week of everything you have accomplished it's a great motivator.

Get out of your comfort zone! Do things that initially feel uncomfortable and different and eventually they will become easy for you. That's a sign of your comfort zone – and you - growing.

Always be a moving target. Continually take action and keep up the momentum. Make it hard for your competition to stay with you and always be doing something different.

Place a value on your own time. Recognise when it makes sense for you to do something and when it doesn't. Understand the most valuable use of your time and delegate those activities/tasks of least value.

Understand the difference between cost and value. Some things in life cost a lot of money; some cost very little or are free. You need to look at what each gives you and weigh up the value you get from each. I know that some of the most expensive things I have paid for have given me the greatest value.

Continually educate yourself. Listen to, read about & watch other successful people and learn from their successes and their mistakes.

Work with a mentor or coach. This will increase your chance of success by giving you accountability and a successful system to follow that the mentor has used themselves or that a coach has taught many others to use.

Systemise your business so it can run without you on a day-to-day basis. The goal should be to go from employment to self-employment to being a true business owner.

Finally, have fun, take more time out, go on holidays and ensure you work on your health and fitness so that you can enjoy the fruits of your labours for as long as possible!

Recommended reading...

Here is a reminder of the titles that I have referred to in this book, and highly recommend you read:

Rich Dad, Poor Dad by Robert Kiyosaki

The E-Myth Revisited by Michael Gerber

Feel the fear & do it anyway by Susan Jeffers

The Dip by Seth Godin

Goals by Brian Tracy

HMO Property Success by Nick Fox

Testimonials

"I have known Neil for more than 15 years and have seen him develop immensely over that time, particularly in the last five years of his property investing journey. Not many people have the ability, desire and determination to become financially free by the age of 30, starting from very humble beginnings. However, Neil put in the time and effort and followed the right systems to set himself up for the rest of his life. He is an inspiration to both first-time property investors and seasoned professionals alike, many of whom recognise that Neil has achieved more success in only five years than they have been able to accomplish in their lifetimes.

This book shows what can be achieved if you have a big enough drive to make change happen, as long as you follow the right systems and have a great support network in place. I have no doubt that Neil will continue to develop, not just as a property investor and businessman, but also as an inspiration to others who wish to follow in his footsteps. I look forward to continuing to share and celebrate those achievements alongside Neil and the people that he mentors."

Steve Bolton, Founding Partner, Platinum Partners

"I have known Neil for around six years, during which time I have watched him progress and develop rapidly, both in the property business and in his personal life. He's bright, focused, dedicated and diligent and is someone I often go to myself for advice and to talk over ideas.

On a personal level, Neil is a pleasure to spend time with - his understated manner belies a quiet intelligence and wicked sense of humour! I have great admiration for the way he constantly challenges himself and would highly recommend him as a very capable businessman and property professional."

Sarah Walker, Writer and former Presenter of BBC1's 'To Buy Or Not To Buy'

"Neil is one of those people that instantly makes you feel at ease in his company and so it comes naturally to build confidence and trust. Unlike so many people in the property market today, there are no easy schemes or get rich quick stories from Neil, but just practical, solid advice and guidance from someone who rolled up his sleeves and learned what to do and what not to do as he implemented his plan to become a successful property investor.

I first met Neil four years ago when, as a mentor, he helped to start me off with my own property investment strategy. Since that time his unlimited energy, crystal clear sense of purpose, extensive knowledge and passion for achieving success in both property and personal development have been a constant inspiration to me. I am also very happy to count Neil as a true personal friend, always ready to help. "

Chris Tapp, former Vice President, International Distributor Marketing & Sales, Allergan EMEA

A Message from Neil

I hope you have enjoyed reading my book. I have tried to make it as simple as possible and really tell you my story since wanting to get involved with property through to the present day. Hopefully it has given you some ideas, inspiration, thoughts and information which you may be able to use for your own circumstances. Whether you are thinking of starting in property or have already begun to build a portfolio the idea is that anyone could take something from this book and use it for your own benefit.

Since writing the book I have already received numerous emails and contact requests from people that are looking for help with their own property investment activities or are seeking to invest in or with someone that is successful in their own sector. Please do get in touch with me through my website if you have any questions or comments regarding anything I have written about in the book including passive investment opportunities, property franchising, mentoring etc, etc. If you have some of your own plans, ideas or opportunities and would like my input then please drop me a line. If I can't help directly, I would hope to be able to point you in the right direction and make any introductions or referrals that you may be looking for.

My website is kept up to date with various blog posts and links to my social media sites so please take a look and get in touch.

To find out more about Neil and his latest projects,
please visit his website at:

www.neilmansell.com

Lightning Source UK Ltd.
Milton Keynes UK
UKOW06f2307200817
307545UK00001B/33/P

9 780956 880505